PRAISE FOR *DESTINY IS NOT HEREDITARY*

Dr. Grossi is that guy who makes you believe that no matter where you come from, no matter the odds against you, if you want it, you can do it! He acts on intuition, which can be a good thing and a bad thing! The good thing is, if he sees a vision and wants it, there is nothing that will stand in his way. He will get what he needs to make it happen and jump in with both feet. He learns what works and what doesn't because, like he always says, you can't get anywhere if you don't at least try.

He is a wonderful family man that always puts his wife and children first. He also loves shoes—you will always find him in shoes that match his outfits, including his laces! One day, a patient loved Dr. Grossi's shoes so much that Doctor surprised the patient by buying him the same exact pair!

He reminds me of Sour Patch Kid candy sometimes. When challenges and stress arrive, he can get a lil' sour, which shows us he's human, but he almost always realizes it and he can be a very sweet individual.

—ANGIE TIDWELL

For me, Dr. Grossi has been a life changer! When I first met Dr. Grossi, I was a crew member at a local restaurant. He saw something in me I was unaware of. He asked me time and again to come work for him because he saw me as a genuine soul with the ability to connect with people.

For almost three years, he continued to ask despite my constant, insecure rejections. Talk about persistence—to be able to see a light in someone who can't even see it themselves, and not give up for three years!

I finally gave in, and since then, he has continued to mentor me not only in his business, but in my personal life, and with family and friends. He even helped me with finances so I could become a first-time homebuyer.

Our relationship is far beyond company owner and employee. It comes from him seeing a light, or spark, in me that he's committed to feeding so it continues to burn brighter and stronger.

—XADIUS WARDEN

I have had the pleasure to work with Dr. Grossi for almost a year. I have been in the dental field for nearly twenty-four years. I have worked in many states and have worked with a large spectrum of general dentists as well as specialists. I have always taken what I have learned from each office and made it my own. Until I met Dr. Grossi, though, I hadn't worked with a doctor that wanted me to better myself for me and my family. He has shown me that I am in control of my future, and for the first time in nearly forty years, I am learning to invest in myself. Building a strong support system and eliminating small stresses helps me focus on the things I can control versus the ones I can't. Dr. Grossi is a mentor to me and I aspire to have half the determination he possesses.

—SHERRY STOUTENBURG

My dad Bobby Grossi. Two words "my hero." My dad has been a huge part of who I am today. He is my biggest inspiration. He inspired me to become a writer. He is the best dad I could ask for. He is truly an amazing person. My father has this amazing drive, he always works hard for his family. He is a great person. He worked so hard for htis book and I couldn't be more proud.

xoxo – your first princess,

—ANDELINA

DESTINY IS NOT HEREDITARY

DR. BOBBY J. GROSSI

DESTINY
IS NOT
HEREDITARY

HOW BECOMING A BETTER YOU IMPACTS OTHERS

Published by Advantage, Charleston, South Carolina.
Member of Advantage Media Group.

ADVANTAGE is a registered trademark, and the Advantage colophon is a trademark of Advantage Media Group, Inc.

Printed in the United States of America.

10 9 8 7 6 5 4 3 2 1

ISBN: 978-1-642250-59-6
LCCN: 2018956913

Cover design by George Stevens.
Layout design by Megan Elger.

This publication is designed to provide accurate and authoritative information in regard to the subject matter covered. It is sold with the understanding that the publisher is not engaged in rendering legal, accounting, or other professional services. If legal advice or other expert assistance is required, the services of a competent professional person should be sought.

Advantage Media Group is proud to be a part of the Tree Neutral® program. Tree Neutral offsets the number of trees consumed in the production and printing of this book by taking proactive steps such as planting trees in direct proportion to the number of trees used to print books. To learn more about Tree Neutral, please visit **www.treeneutral.com**.

Advantage Media Group is a publisher of business, self-improvement, and professional development books and online learning. We help entrepreneurs, business leaders, and professionals share their Stories, Passion, and Knowledge to help others Learn & Grow. Do you have a manuscript or book idea that you would like us to consider for publishing? Please visit **advantagefamily.com** or call **1.866.775.1696**.

*This book is dedicated to Joe Grossi
and Roger Dale Choate, the two male role models in
my life. They both molded me in totally different ways,
but I am forever blessed to know them
and call them family.*

TABLE OF CONTENTS

ACKNOWLEDGMENTS

I would like to thank my beautiful wife, Sabrina, for making me a better man every day. I am so blessed to have you by my side in this journey of life. It is amazing to have the love of my life and best friend all in the same person!

I also would like to thank my beautiful children, Brayden, Andelina, and Zandria. You allow me to dream and have made me so proud as your father. You all are my inspirations and push me every day to be the best version of myself I can be. I hope I have blessed you half as much as you have blessed me.

I would like to thank my mother, Linda Grossi, my brother, Jim Grossi, and my little twin sister, Gina McArdle. You all have supported me and taught me a lot.

Thank you to Antionette Grossi, my grandmother, and Joe Grossi, my grandfather. Thank you for believing in me and feeding me all that pasta. I was so blessed to have you by my side growing up.

Thank you to the Choate family—Roger, Sharon, Shandelle, and Angel. You have all stuck by my side since I was eleven years old. No matter what happened in my life, you never turned your back on me. I am forever grateful and blessed to have you in my life. Thanks for all the support and love.

Thank you to Chris Swanson, for motivating me to become the best I can be.

Thank you, Terry Sippell, for helping me finish the book and pushing me to become a better leader every day.

Thank you to my family at Grossi Dental and Wellness. You have supported all my visions and dreams. Without you all working your tail off for me, nothing would be possible. I appreciate each and every one of you.

And finally, thank you to all my patients and friends who have supported me in my career. I truly am blessed to have all of you and would not be the person I am today without your support!

PREFACE
Changing One Life at a Time

I am one of the most fortunate people in this world, but my journey did not always appear that way.

We all have challenges that in some ways may be incomprehensible to someone else. But no matter the obstacle in your way, you can find a solution to push you through to higher ground. When you dig deep, you can do anything you set your mind to.

My daughter Andelina once made me a Father's Day painting with the phrase "Never go downstairs, always go up," on it. When I asked her what she meant by that, she told me, "Dad, nobody wants to stay at the bottom of something, they are always looking for a way to go to a higher place. Even though it is harder going up and it may hurt at times, you need to just go up the stairs to a higher place. Oh, by the way, Dad, do it one obstacle at a time."

"One Obstacle at a Time" by Andelina Grossi, Father's Day 2016

"Cupcake" by Zandria Grossi, Father's Day 2016

The funny thing is, this message from Andelina, who was twelve at the time, stopped me in my tracks. I was so impressed that she saw life that way, and she was right. I realized that day that my daughter was watching me and listening to me, and that I had a profound impact on her growth and development. Whatever I did, positively or negatively, would shape her in one way or another. My hope, of course, was that my influence would always be positive.

I learned a valuable lesson from my daughter that day. That lesson? We can learn from *everyone* we encounter. We have a responsibility to understand that life is bigger than us, and we need to be aware of how the things we say and do impact other people. We can all be ambassadors of change when we decide to accept responsibility for ourselves and take accountability for our actions and own our power.

My hope is that you will take something from this book that inspires you to look first inside yourself, then beyond, to make a positive change not only in your own life, but in the lives of everyone you encounter.

My personal mission is to make the greatest positive impact or difference with everyone I come across. From my free dental days, to motivational speaking, to writing a book for all of you to read, I want to be the difference maker.

I strongly believe that there is nothing more important in life than family. I want to show my children and family that anything is possible with hard work, commitment, and passion. You can choose to be a dot in life and forgotten, or you can be something bigger and make a difference.

What do you want your legacy to be? How do you want to be remembered?

I want to be remembered as a man who gave everything he had to his family. A man who had integrity, was genuine and honest, and who went the extra mile to make a difference not only in his family's life, but in his community.

Everyone can make an impact. It can start with just one random act of kindness, a simple hello, or a smile.

It starts with ONE.

One thought.

One vision.

One voice.

One step.

One way.

One reason to make a difference: changing one life at a time.

CHAPTER 1

Blamer or Seeker— Which Are You?

From my experience, there are two kinds of people in the world—those who make excuses and blame others for their outcomes or misfortunes, and those who seek the answers to improve their outcomes and guide them to a better fate or destiny. Which are you?

If you are a person who makes excuses, maybe you were programmed that way by a learned behavior in your family. The good news is that you can change. The family you were born into molded you, but you can break that mold and start anew.

Start by looking deep within yourself for the answer. Think of where you are today and how you got there. Do you know? Did you or someone else determine your fate or the path you are on?

You need to realize that it's all about the choices you make that determine your path. Your actions and discipline determine your fate because your life is your own. Don't blame someone else for it or live based on someone else's expectations. Own it and grow from it.

In Flint, Michigan, where I was born and raised, and where I now have my own family and my own business, I have been around a lot of people who think they are broke because their family is broke, because their parents are broke. Granted, the economy is less than ideal in Flint since the automakers left, but I didn't let that stop me—no one should.

We have all seen people who tend to follow how they were raised. Alcoholics and drug users commonly blame family circumstances: "I'm a drug user because my dad was," or, "I'm an alcoholic because my mom was." Poverty levels, addictions, and other undesirable traits go unchanged for generations because of culture blame that is fostered over the years.

I'm here to tell you this: nonsense. You can change any path you want to change regardless of how it starts or what it looks like over time.

Most people tend to conform to society's beliefs about what is socially acceptable and do things that their friends and families want them to do. We are trained from a very young age about what is acceptable and what is not, based on others' beliefs. Typically, people are either too scared to change their path because of the fear of not being loved or of being judged harshly. I also believe that some may be afraid to own their lives because they are afraid to fail, leaving no one but themselves to blame. Finally, some just don't understand that living life according to their own rules is even an option.

It's amazing to me how many times people call others sellouts because they chose a different path than the person making that statement or the path everyone expected them to follow. I have heard so many times, "He forgot where he came from," or, "She forgot where she came from." Did they? Or did they just do something you couldn't do? Did they decide on a new destiny and not conform to the culture they were surrounded by? Many times, we are warned, "Be careful who you hang around with—you can become just like them." I would rather put a positive spin on that same thought: know who you hang around with, and surround yourself with people better than you, and who have a better situation emotionally and financially. You may just become like them.

I am an example of the belief that your destiny is not hereditary. I was raised by a single mother in Flint. She made a whopping $24,000 a year and had three children. My dad never supported the family financially when my parents were together, and he left when I was two years old. Every time my mom asked for more money, he would threaten to leave the state and not pay child support. Any person from Flint understands the situation I am talking about. A lot of people growing up in Flint have a very similar story.

My dad was also an addict, and he fought with my mom every day. He didn't know the first thing about raising children. I can remember having dinner at his place, with wife number two, and I started choking on food. Instead of being concerned about me choking, he got annoyed. He got up from the table and hit me so hard over the head with a spoon that it broke. The good news is that I stopped choking, but I'll never forget the embarrassment I felt with everyone around the table laughing at me. I felt as though I had done something wrong, and the shame was awful.

Growing up, my dad never said he loved me, and I truly believe he wanted nothing to do with us. He would pick me and my siblings up on the weekends because he had to, not because he wanted to. When I was with him, I would count the hours until I could go home. My dad was a very selfish man who only cared about his own life.

While my mom worked hard to provide for us, she was also very toxic. She was always depressed and played the victim. Shopping was her way of filling the void in her heart or covering her pain. She had very poor money habits and continually spent out of emotion, not out of need. We never had enough money, but my mom would never own the fact that she was a major part of the reason we didn't. It was always someone else's fault.

(Left to Right) Me, my mom, sister Gina, and my brother Jim, 1978

Despite her unhappiness, I know my mom loved us and would do anything for us. But her problems became ours. She never shielded us from the adult drama in her life, and of course, children are not emotionally equipped to handle adult problems. No matter what, she came first and we came second.

My brother and sister and I were raised more by our grandparents than our own parents. Most of my guidance growing up came from them or from my wife's family.

A STEP IN *MY* DIRECTION

I can remember growing up and marching to the beat of my own drum. Out of anger and frustration, I made up my mind to never follow in the footsteps of my parents. Every decision I made growing up, I would ask myself, "What would my dad do?" and then I would do the total opposite. I think most people would just feel sorry for themselves and behave based on the examples that were set, but not me. I took my dad's negatives and turned them into positives. I took all his failures and learned from them like they were my own.

One of my first steps in choosing a totally different path came when I was eighteen years old. My twin sister and I changed our last names to my mother's maiden name—something my brother had already done a few years prior. I never wanted to be someone who honored my father.

I was proud to take the name of my grandfather, because I loved and respected him and he was always there for me. His death as a result of throat cancer was incredibly difficult for me, and it was then that I decided to further honor him by going into the field of medicine.

My wife, Sabrina, has pushed me daily to become a better version of myself, and she is one of the major reasons I became a dentist. Before we married, we talked about our future lives together and possibly having a family. When I brought up medical school, Sabrina, being a nurse, understood that it would be difficult for me to be a medical doctor *and* have a balanced family life. So she suggested dentistry as an option. That way I wouldn't have to be "married to a pager." (For the much younger readers, a pager was a device you wore on your hip. When someone needed to reach you, they dialed up the pager and left their phone number for you to call. Today, thankfully, we all have cell phones.) I could still be in medicine to honor my grandfather and be a family man.

I now do motivational speaking so that I can share my message of hope that *anyone* can achieve what they set their mind to. That is my purpose in this book. To share my story and change the life of at least one person, to energize them. I want to tell people how to break the mold, to reject the bad seeds and choose the best seed that has been planted in their life, then grow strong and plant a different, better seed in someone else.

I spend a lot of time coaching and mentoring youth and young entrepreneurs, because I want to help nurture them and show them the way. For those who come from broken homes, those without guidance, I have a message: It is not how you are raised, it is what you want to become. No one has control over your life, they only have a part of it. They can't make you become you, they can only influence what you become. I am a dentist, but it does not mean any of my children will ever be dentists. I might have an influence, but it is up to them to decide their own path.

PLANT A NEW SEED

I did not have a lot of money growing up, but I did not let that stop me from grinding away to become a dentist. I did not rely on others to make my dreams happen. Life does not work that way. You

> **You can't rely on others to pay your way or to create your path for you.**

can't rely on others to pay your way or to create your path for you. Have you ever wondered why cities stay broke, or cultures never change? How many people have you seen living off of government assistance turn into millionaires? That is not likely, because the universe rewards dreamers—it rewards people who go get what is rightfully theirs.

People who are raised in poverty have a hard time breaking free. Why? Because of the deeply rooted beliefs that have been planted in their life, a generation of "can't" culture embedded in them. But you can plant a new seed and change your destiny with one step in a different direction.

There is hope out there! If you want something badly enough, you can get it, and you don't have to do it alone! People will always be there to help you. Sometimes you need to make a stand to change your course, and it may feel like you're alone, but you don't have to be.

I clearly remember a pivotal moment in my life when I was in my last year of dental school. I did not pass my exam, and I was totally devastated. I did not want to go home and tell my wife I failed. She had made so many sacrifices to put me through dental school, and I didn't have the heart to tell her things were about to get harder.

Instead, I went to the one place I thought was a safe place to land, my mom's. I walked into her house and she was sitting in her chair in the corner. I sat down, and she started to tell me all of her problems and how sad she was. I listened and counseled and gave her a sympathetic ear.

As I started to leave, I think it dawned on her that I wanted to talk to her, because she asked me why I came over. Crying, I explained that I had failed my exam, I was $200,000 in debt, and I didn't know what I was going to do. I told her I just needed support from her. Her response was nothing I expected.

She said she didn't have time for my problems, since she had problems of her own, and she told me I just needed to toughen up. I remember sitting there feeling just awful, not knowing what to do, needing nothing but sympathetic support and maybe a hug. I needed my mother's love and tenderness but instead got a cold shoulder.

I made the hard decision that day to walk away from the people who didn't add any positivity or value to my life. I decided to focus solely on my wife and my child and go forge my own path, make my dreams come true, without my mom or dad. While I initially felt alone, I had my wife, my child, and my wife's whole family pulling for me. That day, the day

I realized my power, is the day that forever changed my path.

A few years later, when I graduated dental school, I was the first in my family to go to grad school and the first to get my doctorate. What was not the norm then may eventually be the norm in my family. You have the ability to do the same thing.

Go make your dreams happen. You determine your path. You can break ground that has never been broken in your family before. You can be the one who changes the destiny of family members who follow in the path behind you. You can make the difference.

Look at the life of a seed. First, you plant it in the wet, dark, and cold ground. Nothing happens for a few months, then eventually, the seed grows internally and breaks through all the resistance from the ground and gets set free. It sees the whole world, it becomes self-sufficient, it relies only on wind and water to reproduce. That one seed can lead to a whole generation of that plant.

You will need wind and water throughout your journey, and you will need people to help you, but you can change your path by making one decision. You can plant a new seed and change your destiny. Live for you, not your family. Live to become the best you can be, not what others want you to be. You are the difference maker. Your destiny is determined by your actions, not anyone else's.

DETERMINE YOUR DESTINY

- Plant your seed to greatness.

- The universe rewards people who make a difference and have faith in the outcome.

- The greatest inventors were the ones who believed in themselves and changed the path of things.

- Your destiny is controlled by your beliefs and actions, no one else's.

CHAPTER 2
It's Not Just About You

What do you think about every day when you wake up? Do you think you can make a difference in this world? Do you think that your actions affect other people? Do you even know the amount of power you have with every decision you make?

Most people going through life have no idea the role they play in others' lives. They tend to either ignore the fact or go through life unaware that every decision they make affects others in some way.

A NEW MINDSET

Everything you do in life is not just about you. Most selfish people think that is the case, but it is far from the truth. If you want to become a leader or a top one-percenter, you've got to change that mindset.

The new mindset has to be that nothing is about *me*; it is about *everyone else*. It is about living a self*less* life instead of a self*ish* life. Every decision you make can change the path of several other people involved. No matter what you do in life, you impact others. Your decisions affect your family, community, coworkers, work or business, employees, and even vendors.

Let's take the example of my decision to go to dental school. I made the choice because it's what *I* wanted to do, but I did not consider the impact it would have on others. But here's how my decision affected others. First, it put my wife's life on hold. She had to work her tail off on third shift in a cath lab, a job for which she was on call 24/7. When she wasn't at work, she was raising our son. For the first two years of his life, I got to spend very little time with him. I'd wake him up at 4:30 in the morning to take him to my in-law's house until my wife could pick him up there. My selfish decision had a huge impact on many other people.

Now let's look at my wife's decision. She chose to support my dream and considered everyone *but* herself. She worked late to enable her to be with our son during the day. She worked hard to financially support us while I went to school and even shielded me from the stress and strain of the endless bills coming in. Her selfless decision made it possible for me to pursue my dream.

Sabrina. My beautiful wife, best friend, and inspiration.

Her decision to support me during that time affects people far beyond our family today. As a business owner, I provide jobs to many people, which in turn affects their families. I order supplies from vendors, which affects their lives. I help my patients feel better both physically and mentally. That helps keep their bodies healthy, which affects their lives.

Since the business has been so successful, I'm able to contribute generously to my community and my church. My wife will never have to work outside the home again, and my practice allows me to spend a lot of time with my family, affecting the lives of my children. My wife's selfless decision affected many, many lives, most especially mine.

YOUR GREATER IMPACT

Every one of us has a greater impact than we think. Some of us have greater impact than others, but we *all* can, and do, impact lives.

I love the comparison of a boulder hitting water versus a pebble hitting water. Yes, when a boulder hits water, initially there is a bigger splash, and initially the wave is more powerful, but at the end of the journey the waves take the shape and flow of the water until it hits its end point. The same is true for a pebble. It creates a wave, maybe not as powerful in the beginning and less noticeable, but it ripples out and affects what's around it. This stands true for you. Big or small, you make an impact on others every day.

Too often people go through life focusing only on their own needs and wants. They do not look at others' lives and consider how their actions affect another person's life. As a leader of a company, the look on my face or the words that come out of my mouth can change the mood of an employee. It can change their day, or it can change the way they look at life for the positive or negative. I remember that I can be part of a solution, or I can be part of a problem.

If I walk through my practice and only point out things I see that are wrong, then I'm only thinking of myself. That is *not* the right way to inspire people and make them feel part of the team. If I walk through and point out the things that are right and make suggestions on how to improve the things that are not, then I'm part of the solution instead of being part of the problem.

Do you think of putting a smile on *your* face first, or someone else's face first? Do you ever hold a door open for a complete stranger? Do you ever perform any kind of random act of kindness? If not, why not? We have no idea what other people are going through, nor do most of us care, but imagine if we all did.

We have no idea what other people are going through, nor do most of us care, but imagine if we all did.

17

Imagine what a wonderful world we would live in if we always considered others.

The Christian thing is to do unto others what we would want done to ourselves. How do you feel when someone smiles at you? How do you feel when someone tells you, you look good? How do you feel when someone goes above and beyond for you or your loved ones? The next time someone makes you feel good, recognize that they have had an impact on you, and then pass that on—make an impact on someone else.

You have the power to make a difference in someone else's day, someone else's life. Every time you wake up, think of being a difference maker. Realize that the impact you'll have on any one person can ultimately impact several hundred or even thousands of people. You can change the way the world looks at things.

Look at Colin Kaepernick. He decided on a big scale not to stand for the national anthem. Whether you agree with him or not, he made a stance for what he believed in. He may have changed forever the way the NFL is viewed, the way Colin himself is viewed, and for some, even the way the national anthem is viewed. He affected not only his own life, but several million others by just one decision. To stand or not to stand.

YOUR LIFE MATTERS

Let's take another example of how a selfish decision can affect others. Suicide.

Most of the time when someone commits a selfish act of suicide, they only think about themselves. They are not thinking about the other people they affect or leave behind. They are so lost in their own life that they can't even see others. Their one decision to end their life will forever change the loved ones they left behind. That one act affects children, colleagues, friends, and family members. The person who committed suicide does not suffer, but forever their family or friends will have to deal with the pain of losing them. They may wonder what they could have done to make a difference in saving that person's life. Did the person committing suicide even know the impact they could have had or the impact they did have? Probably not, because if they had considered others first, they would never have made that choice.

No matter what you are going through when you are reading this, or no matter where you have been, people can and will help you.

Whether you are a leader or a homeless person, your life matters and the decisions you make will impact others. Remember that and you can begin to live your life to help make the lives of others better.

Life is, and always will be, bigger than you. Without you in it, the path of the world would be different. Go make that difference!

YOUR ACTIONS HAVE IMPACT

- Think before you speak. Your words can wound or they can heal.
- Remember that your actions can have a major impact on others.
- The decision you make today can have lasting effects on others, now and in the future.

CHAPTER 3

Dreaming Is for Winners

Have you ever dreamed of what it would be like to win the lottery? When you think of all the things you could do with the winnings, you enter a state of euphoria, allowing your mind to just dream. That's the power of dreaming.

The kind of dreams I'm talking about are those in which you envision your future. Your dreams will allow you to harness the energy of the universe through your thoughts. Dreams can drive your passion, give you a vision of your purpose, help get you to another level. Dreams can show you what a better tomorrow looks like. Perhaps best of all, they can help you have happiness and hope.

Envisioning what you want for yourself, what your future looks like, can be the most energizing thing you can do for yourself. When you allow yourself to dream, your mind becomes limitless—there is nothing to stop the creative energy inside of you.

Dreams release a positive energy in your body and allow you to feel a happiness that cannot be matched. When you dream, you are relating to your desires. You are dreaming about what makes *you* happy, not what someone else thinks will make you happy.

DREAMS WORK ON A SUBCONSCIOUS LEVEL

Allowing yourself to dream can help your subconscious mind work on your behalf. It can help you imagine ways of overcoming barriers, helping you get a clearer vision of how to achieve your desires. What do you truly want to accomplish in your life? What do you want for others? By envisioning the possibilities, you can overcome any obstacle.

By envisioning the possibilities, you can overcome any obstacle.

For example, when I was a child I dreamed of living financially free, not worrying about how I was going to pay my bills like my mother did. I also dreamed of having a stable family with my wife by my side and having fun with my children. Every time I committed to something, I first would dream to envision a better tomorrow and allow myself to live in that moment until it felt real.

When you dream, you allow yourself to be free from distraction. You are showing yourself what you truly desire. When you desire something, your conscious and subconscious mind can then work on your behalf to help you get to the promised land.

One of my greatest desires was to be a dentist and to change the way people view dentistry. I spent countless hours envisioning what my practice would be like: what my staff would be like, what type of patients we would help, everything in great detail. I also dreamed of eliminating the fear or phobia people have about dentists and changing the way medical doctors view dentists. You see, dentists are doctors, too. Dentists graduate with a doctor of dental surgery (DDS) degree, whereas medical doctors graduate with a doctor of medicine (MD) degree. I dream that one day dentists and doctors of medicine will work together to remove patients' insecurities and treat them as a whole person, not as separate health issues.

When I finally became a dentist, I remembered all the dreams I had and how I wanted them to turn out. I currently run a successful practice focusing on the total wellness of my patients through a healthy mouth. I and my terrific staff are taking the fear out of dentistry by actively educating every patient on the overall health benefits of good oral hygiene. We help patients understand that they play an active part in helping control issues like diabetes, hypertension, cardiovascular disease, stroke, and even dementia and Alzheimer's.

When patients understand the overall benefits of dentistry, the "I hate the dentist" mentality starts to change. We become a partner and advocate, which shifts the perspective from enemy to friend. While we have made great strides in this arena, we still have a long way to go. Dreams rarely become reality overnight.

I truly believe dreams are the Holy Spirit, or an outside energy working on your behalf. It is very important to listen to your dreams. They will help guide you down the path you were meant to go on. They can drive you to reach for a better life than what you have or want.

My beautiful children, Zandria (2 yrs), Brayden (8 yrs),
and Andelina (5 yrs). (2009)

Children have imaginary friends and can play all alone. They create new games to play just to entertain themselves. My brother and I even made up football games and dreamt of what it would feel like to win the Super Bowl. I had a dream of winning a World Series title as a baseball player. I dreamed I was the hero in the game. I imagined the team lifting me on their shoulders. I could hear the crowd chanting my name.

Of course, I am not a professional athlete. I did, however, get to play in a World Series—the Connie Mack World Series, in which teens from across the United States, Canada, and Puerto Rico compete. I pitched against Puerto Rico, and my team took third place in the nation. I guess my dream wasn't specific enough.

YADDA, YADDA, YADDA

Your dream must be big—so big that even if you fall short you're still closer to getting what you want. God wants us to reach our greatest potential, and you don't get there by dreaming small. The bigger the dream, the more you allow yourself to stretch, which turns into growth. It also allows the universe to align for you.

Why do some people dream and others don't? Even though people know the power of dreaming, they stop doing it. They start doubting themselves, and say, "This is my life. I have made my bed. I can't dream. I have responsibilities, I have bills to pay," yadda, yadda, yadda.

Most people who say those things are not happy people. They are stressed and bogged down with everyday life. They are blocked by negativity. They have forgotten what it was like to be a little child. At the end of their journey, they will have impacted few others and missed out on of a lot of opportunities that came their way.

Over time, it's easy to conform to the masses and live life according to what other people want instead what we want. When we allow that to happen, we stop the growth of our mind and we block outside energy from working on our behalf. We block all the creative energy that the Lord has given us.

Your dreams will allow you to harness the energy of the universe through your thoughts. Dreams can drive your passion, they can give you a vision of your purpose, they can help get you to another level. Dreams can show you what a better tomorrow looks like. Perhaps best of all, they can help you have happiness and hope.

HARNESS THE POWER OF YOUR DREAMS

- Never forget to dream.
- Don't ignore your dreams.
- Write down your dreams and read them out loud twice a day.
- Allow your subconscious mind to be a bad mamma jamma on your behalf.

CHAPTER 4

Discover Your Purpose

What does the word "purpose" mean? Purpose is the *reason* something is done, or that something is created. Do you know your purpose? Do you know why you are here on Earth? Do you know how to find your purpose?

When I think about purpose, there is no better example of someone who had a clearer purpose than Jesus Christ. His purpose was to teach us the Lord's way and to die for us so that all of our sins would be forgiven. He went through life being shunned and ridiculed. He even went through life with people telling him, "You are not God's Son." Whether you believe in the Lord or not is irrelevant. I have my beliefs, and you, of course, have your own. For the sake of the story, though, I will continue.

Think of how hard it was for Jesus to fulfill his purpose. He was knocked down, spit on, beaten with whips, and had to carry the incredibly heavy burden of his purpose. Can you imagine if he had not continued, if he had not fulfilled his purpose? Life as we know it would forever be changed. Jesus continued no matter how hard the struggle was to fulfill his purpose, dying for all of us. Doesn't sound fun, but he did it anyway, because his purpose was clear.

To be successful in life, you need to know what your purpose is. Without purpose, you do not even know where you should be going and may not be fulfilling your role here on this earth. Everything you do in life should align with your purpose.

The two greatest days of your life are when you were born and the day you find out what your purpose is. It's hard to keep going in life without purpose, without working for or toward something, but when you *do* know, everything becomes crystal clear. Your life has a new meaning, a new reason for doing what you do. It has purpose.

Your purpose could be as simple as being the best teammate in a company, or the biggest difference maker in technology. It could be being the best teacher at a school, or even changing the way education is done. Everyone's purpose is not equal, and too often, people go through life without even searching or trying to find their purpose.

HOW TO FIND YOUR PURPOSE

Many people go through life feeling lost or feeling that something is missing in their life. They just go through the motions hoping that one day the part that is missing will come to them. They want a deeper meaning or connection but are not sure how to find it.

I did not know my purpose until I was nearly forty years old. I thought my purpose was to make the greatest impact in dentistry, but that was not it. That is not why I was called here on this Earth. My purpose is to try and make the greatest positive difference with every single person I come in contact with. Whether that is through motivational speaking, writing books, coaching sports, being a husband and father, or holding a door for a perfect stranger.

So how does one find their purpose? First, you need to go toward the things you want and start removing the things you don't want. Find out what makes you tick or smile and focus on that. Really get to know what makes you happy—what it is that feeds your body with an energy you can't explain—and then continue down that road. Purpose cannot be taught. It is more of an inner feeling and awakening to the emotions in one's own body. It's an awareness of who you are and what you value. You need to really know your wants and your desires to help you find your purpose.

If you're struggling to find your purpose, try new things. Take action over your life. If you want to write a book, write it. If you want to be a good mother, define what that means and then do everything you can to be that. If you want to leave your job, leave it. Take control of your life and *take action!* Watch the universe open up to you and help you find your purpose.

Your heart is your guide in finding your purpose. Get out of your own head. Do what you love and what inspires you. When you are happy, energy flows through your body and you become a better and stronger you.

Your heart is your guide in finding your purpose.

By doing what you love, you will gain insights on what makes you happy and what brings you the most joy. That is closer to your purpose than you think.

Too often, people think their purpose is limited to one thing. That is not always the case. Your purpose can involve multiple things. My purpose is to make a difference in everyone's life I come in contact with. I am a father, husband, dentist, motivational speaker, author, coach, mentor—and all-around nice guy. All the things I do line up with my purpose to have the greatest positive impact on people.

You also need to find what you're passionate about. If you live life with passion, you are aware of the wonderful things in life, and the universe will help lead you to your purpose.

Your purpose is something that energizes you beyond belief and fulfills you. You don't have to get paid for the job you are doing, because you are so happy and fulfilled doing it. You get rewarded with the energy. This happens to me every time I speak in public or help inspire people.

Dentistry allows me the freedom to achieve my purpose, or to live a life with a purpose. I am so blessed to have a profession where I can have the greatest impact on a person. I can affect their health, their emotional well-being, and even their family members. I also have the freedom to do motivational speaking and write books.

GET OUT OF YOUR OWN WAY

Too often people know what they really want but can't get out of their own way to fulfill their happiness. But if you look deep within yourself you will discover what makes you happy.

If you are always on the lookout for your purpose, if you are open to change and seek an answer, you will find it. Your body is an amazing tool, something we were all blessed with. If you listen to what energizes your body, if you allow yourself to be totally free with no barriers, you will find your purpose.

FINDING YOUR PURPOSE

- Find your passion; that will lead you to your purpose.

- Get to know yourself and what you want and desire.

- Once you know your purpose, test it and see how happy you become.

- Make sure everything you do aligns with that purpose.

- Go conquer the world. Live life to the fullest— that is what we were meant to do.

CHAPTER 5

Power of Your Thoughts

There is an old phrase that you eat the fruit of your words (Proverbs 18:21). I personally think you mirror the power of your thoughts.

Let me give you an example of what I mean. When you are happy, you have happy thoughts. You go through the day with a song in your heart, a dance in your step. Everything has a certain buzz, or energy, or passion—you feel closer to your purpose. When you are happy, endorphins are released—these aid in healing and minimize the stress in your life.

Every song on the radio, is a happy one. All you hear or want to hear are happy thoughts, great ideas, things that have positive energy. You may even want to sing along, out loud: "This song is the bomb!" Think of how great a day you have when you are happy.

Now flip that around. When you are sad the opposite happens, because your thoughts are sad. We have all lost a loved one or broken up with someone we loved. When you listen to the radio when you are sad, all you hear is love songs about breakups—every song on the radio reminds you of all the pain you are going through. It is like somebody keeps dumping salt on those open wounds. When you're sad, you don't hear the same songs on the radio that you were dancing to the other day. You are only open to the power of sadness, which is your dominant thought.

If your thoughts have all the power, then why don't people just change the way they think? The answer is simple—I have no idea. Maybe people have a fear of failure or get stuck in their old ways. Maybe people do what others want them to do instead of doing what they want to do. If you truly want to grow, you need to change your thought processes first—and then the rest will follow.

A DIFFERENT POINT OF VIEW

One of the biggest changes I ever made in my fifteen-year dental career was to change the way I thought.

I changed the way I thought about my business, I changed the way I thought about myself, and I changed the way I thought about my staff and the community I live in.

I thought of what it would be like to have a big business, and then I had to change the way I thought about my business: I was not small business, I was big business. Just thinking about my business that way enlarged it in my mind—that was a great start. Think about that for a minute: If someone says you are no big deal, you feel insecure and maybe sad. But if someone says you are great, or you're an important person, you have a sense of pride. Your shoulders go back, your chest puffs out, and you feel happy.

I also changed the way I dressed, which changed the way I mentally viewed myself. Dress for success, fake it to make it—we have all heard those phrases. Well, they work, because they change the way you think about yourself. It is like when you get dressed up to go on a date, you always feel more beautiful or handsome. You have a lot more confidence and feel happy. If you wear sweatpants, you tend to feel lazy or less attractive. You hear people saying, "I'm just bumming it today." Guess what? If you think you're a bum, you're a bum.

I changed the way I thought about my staff. I changed from being all about me to being all about their growth. My perspective changed from me being the center of my practice to them being the center of it. I knew that if I could change them emotionally and mentally, and invest in their future, they would invest in mine and my family's.

And I changed the way I viewed my patients. Instead of me having an ego and approaching my relationships with them as if "I'm the man," I realized that a patient could go anywhere. I realized that I am blessed to even have the ability to help them with their physical and emotional well-being. My patients allow me to be a part of their lives. They allow me to achieve part of my purpose.

In short, I changed the focus from thinking all about *me* to thinking all about *them*. That's the power of your thoughts.

In order for the power of your thoughts to work, you have to feel that you're worthy. You have to have the confidence to know that you were meant for greatness. I was very cynical and pessimistic for many years—I often played victim. I finally realized that to become

You have to have the confidence to know that you were meant for greatness.

someone I wanted to be, I had to change my thoughts about life. To be a success, I had to change myself first.

I used to think my upbringing made me incapable of doing anything. Life was against me. I didn't have money for dental school. I couldn't afford to eat every day. I was broke. I thought life wasn't fair. Students in my class were getting full rides because of their race, or they could live with their parents and stay at home rent free. The funny thing is, I was playing the victim. My thoughts were toxic and controlled my life. I chose my path—no one else chose it for me. I chose to have a child and get married in dental school. I stepped up and owned it.

I began shutting off all negative noise around me. All I allowed in were positive thoughts and ideas. I read inspirational books, listened to inspirational CDs, watched affirmation videos.

I also found mentors and coaches to keep me on track. So many people go through life without a coach. Coaches and mentors are valued for their objectivity and honesty. Plus, they have already had success and can show you all the skills and secrets they used to get you where you want to go. In life, you need to stay humble and learn from the people who have gone ahead of you. Don't reinvent the wheel but learn from your coach and then make it your own. That's part of getting out of your own way—sometimes you have to ask for help.

The fact is, I was preventing my growth by my own doing, no one else's. My dominant thoughts were molding my future. We have the ability through our thoughts to get power from the universe, but I wasn't allowing the power of the universe to work on my behalf.

Once I changed my thoughts, my life changed faster than you can imagine. My confidence soared. My business doubled in a year. And I was starting to reach my God-given potential.

Successful people never think they can't—they think they can. They also tend not to let outside noise of negativity clutter their life. That means limiting exposure to Facebook, not watching reality shows, not watching the negative news. If you control your thoughts to work on your behalf, you are one step closer to reaching your greatness.

Your thoughts inspire emotions, which help inspire your actions in life, which help form your reality.

THE POWER OF YOUR THOUGHTS

- Your thoughts help guide your future.

- Your thoughts can make or break you.

- Your thoughts can give you the power over your life.

- Your thoughts can also destroy you.

- If you think you can, you can. If you think you can't, I promise you, you WON'T.

CHAPTER 6

Change Is *Good*

Growing up in Genesee County in Flint, Michigan, I was taught that change was a bad thing. People would always say how much they hated change, or how change made them nervous or mad. Today I laugh thinking of that. Why do you think cities stay the same for generations? Why do you think people don't grow, or make more money than they did twenty years ago? The answer is simple—because they did *not change*.

I still hear "change is bad" to this day, but when you encounter a challenge or failure that causes you to change your path, usually that change ends up being a good thing.

How many people have you known who stayed in their job because they were afraid to change? People tend to be scared to change jobs or their situation in life even though it is often the right move for them. Yet if they are truly unhappy with some area of their life, they become stale or stagnant.

But lack of growth equates to death. Most people in life have been fired at one time or another, and that kind of sudden change or disappointment hits you right in the gut. It may feel like the world is going to end. But then, as you realize the change ultimately led to a better version of you, you become much happier.

How about someone who has to go on a diet for health reasons? If they don't change their diet or current habits, their life could be cut drastically short. But if they would just accept that change, they would improve their life overall. That change could not only save their life but allow their family to spend more time with them.

STOP BEING THE VICTIM

Why do people refuse to change when that change can lead to great things? Why would people continue to play victim when there are other options? Why do we keep electing people to positions of power when we know that nothing will change?

As a native of Flint, I've known a lot of people who view life as a victim. They never have enough, or the government is wrong, or the automaker GM does not give them enough. That is all victim mentality. What about how blessed people were to have GM around for years and have all those high-paying jobs with great benefits? It was not GM that let people down, it was people who took advantage of the system. People who wanted to get paid without having to work. I worked at GM and I saw this all too well. I witnessed individuals who would drink on the job, clock-in, and then go to the local bar. Many just did the bare minimum to get by. I was personally ostracized because I wanted to not only learn how to master my job but figure out how to do it better. People refused to put forth the effort to improve their lives, and it put the company and the people who worked there at risk. Inability to change led to the crash of the auto industry—in my opinion, that's what devastated Flint.

Let's take a look at some of the nation's poorer cities. Why do you think they're in the position they're in? Most of the time, people blame the government, but their blame is misplaced. We, the people, are the ones who vote people into office. We are the ones who elect governors and mayors. Why do some cities always vote Democrat or Republican? Because that is how it has been for generations. We cannot be surprised that refusing to change, doing the same thing over and over, produces the same results. It takes change to make a difference; it's the lack of change that does not move the ball.

Here's another example of change: Let's say you just broke up with someone—we have all been there. At first you feel like the world is coming to an end—like you have hit rock bottom and there is no way you will ever love again. Once again, playing the victim. But then you start thinking about the other person as a jerk, or you begin to realize how much better off you are without that relationship, or you learn what you did wrong and vow never to do it again. You start to heal from pain. And in the end, the loss of that relationship makes you stronger. Change made you better.

Sometimes change is forced on you. You could lose a loved one suddenly, you could have marriage issues, or you could be fired from a job. However it happens, sometimes forced change is God's way of saving you. Sometimes the forced change makes you see things in a different way and gets you back on track in your life.

The biggest changes in my life have come from an "aha" moment—those moments when I hit rock bottom and don't behave in a way that I'm proud of or when I disappoint people, whether my coworkers, family members, or friends. When I upset people, it causes me to look deep within myself to determine if I am being the person I was meant to be. I ask myself if I'm being the best version of myself or if I'm living in a way that will get me closer to my purpose.

For example, there have been times when I'm doing homework with my children and I'm exhausted. All I want to do is to unwind and relieve some stress, and I respond incorrectly. I get short and project my frustrations on them. It cuts me to the core when my wife shows disappointment in me and my kids look devastated. When that happens, I reframe my thinking immediately. I realize that a true leader shows grace and patience. A true leader responds to stressful situations calmly and realizes that life doesn't always work based on their timetable. It is not wrong to want and have personal time, but it is wrong to project your stress and frustration onto other people.

My wife's disappointment hits me square in the face. That is my a-ha moment, and it causes me to look deep within myself and make a change. Such a-ha moments, I believe, are what causes most people to change. When you become self-aware and see your flaws clearly, you can then determine what changes you want to make. That is how you become the best version of yourself.

In 2008, I had to make a tough decision. I sold my dental company for a whopping $20,000, because every day I worked, I was away from my family, and miserable. I had a long commute that made the time I was away from them even greater, to the point that it was hard for me to be a part of their everyday lives. I was not really getting to see my kids grow and to impact their lives. I knew I had to *jump* and be all in.

I gave up being the owner of a practice and started going to work one day a week as an associate dentist in an area closer to my house. I was broke and afraid that I was going to lose everything. But I also knew that if I didn't make the change, I would lose more than just money. I would lose my most important asset, my family.

To accomplish what I set out to do, I had to reestablish all of my ethical principles, look deep within myself, and make the necessary changes to stop focusing just on myself. I had to broaden my perspective and focus on the bigger picture, which was my family. I had to show strength and confidence even when I was scared of failing. I had to have trust and faith that all my hard work would pay off and show my family that I was committed to our success.

My Purpose and my motivation! (2011)

I stayed the course and with the grace of God and faith bought Gateway Dental, now Grossi Dental and Wellness, the company I have now owned for over ten years. I am now writing books and giving motivational speeches. I have three beautiful children and an amazing wife who makes me better every day. If I had not changed my ways or my path, I would not be where I am today. Change is great!

GET OUT OF YOUR COMFORT ZONE

Imagine where we would be today if the world never changed. Think about technology alone: Where would we be if technology had never evolved, or if advances had not been made in health care?

Change is how advances are made in the world. It's how life improves, it's how cures are found, and it's how we become better versions of ourselves.

Change happens when you get out of your comfort zone and push yourself daily to change. If you stay stagnant, then twenty years will pass you by and you will be left wondering what the hell happened to you and your life. You will still have the mindset of a twenty-year-old but be looking in the mirror at a stranger. Unfortunately, the stranger you will be looking at is yourself.

Too many people stay in their comfort zone because they are so afraid to leave it.

Too many people stay in their comfort zone because they are so afraid to leave it. It might be from a lack of self-confidence or a fear of failure, or because they feel family members are holding them back. Whatever the reason, it's *nonsense*—these are nothing but excuses. If you feel your family is holding you back, take a stance in your life. If you are scared, take action—that's the best way to overcome your fears. If you lack confidence, take baby steps to turn that around. Read self-help books or talk to others—they will help you increase confidence.

If you decide to do something different than what others expect of you, your family may give you some resistance at first, but it will be okay. Sometimes you have to show not only the importance of what you're doing for yourself, but also the benefit your family members will receive by supporting you and helping you achieve your goals. Once you are truly committed to something and explain why, they will be all in with you. People tend to follow leaders, so take the lead in your life. People also love confidence, so be confident in your decisions. When you are driven and confident, your family will follow you and root for you. They sometimes just need to be shown how they will benefit. It's like a team sport: once the players buy into the coach and are shown the promised land, they will run through a wall to win for the team.

If you never leave your comfort zone, it is almost impossible to take you or your business to new heights. If you show a lack of faith in yourself and your business, the universe cannot align on your behalf. Channels won't open up to help you, and eventually your risk meter button stops going off. I liken it to the voice we all have in our head. We hear a voice that tells us what we should be doing or not doing. If we ignore that voice, eventually we never hear it anymore and it goes away. Your vision and dreams—and especially your creative energy—will die if you stay in your comfort zone.

Now I am happy to report that I speak in front of hundreds of people at a time, and I hope to build that number to thousands. In doing so, I am living closer to my purpose. My purpose is to make a difference in everyone's life that I come in contact with, and now I'm doing that on a bigger scale with my motivational speaking. More and more I'm moving toward my ultimate goal of retiring from dentistry and only speaking for a living. Imagine if I had never changed, if I had never taken the initiative to get over my fear of public speaking. I would have missed my calling, my purpose in this world, all because I was scared of change. *Thank God I did not stay in my comfort zone.*

Every time I think of a comfort zone, I think of someone eating with sweatpants on because the elastic band makes them more comfortable. Years go by and they end up weighing twenty more pounds—their size thirty waistband is now size thirty-eight. By staying in their comfort zone, they didn't grow as a better person, they just grew older and unhealthy. That's not living, and that's not living a purpose that impacts others.

What are you going to change about your life right now? How is your change going to affect your life and others?

POINTS TO REMEMBER ABOUT CHANGE

- Change is for people who want to grow.
- Change, and have faith, and everything will work out.
- I promise you, no matter what you think will happen, you will always become a better version of yourself after the change.
- Without change, you don't have growth. All you have in the long run is death.
- Change is how the world becomes better and better.

CHAPTER 7

Commitment vs. Interest

When I was thirteen years old, I was the bat boy for my grandfather's baseball team. Jim Abbott, the one-handed pitcher, was pitching the regional championship game in Marshall, Michigan, to send the Grossi Nationals to the Connie Mack World Series in Farmington, New Mexico. The team he was pitching against was a very arrogant, cocky team from Ypsilanti, Michigan. I remember that team's fans calling Jim names like "duck," and ripping on him for having only one hand. It was the worst sportsmanship I have ever witnessed.

In the bottom of the seventh inning, we were winning by one run, with two outs. Jim was one out away from pitching what would be a winning championship game, shutting up those fans and players. With one strike gone and runners on second and third, Jim grooved a pitch right down the middle and the ump called it a ball. We could not believe it. Everyone was going crazy, and I could see the look of just plain disbelief on Jim's face. He threw one more pitch and the batter got a base hit—and we lost the game.

The worst part of the fiasco was that then the other team ran onto the field, giving us the bird and knocking over our players and fans. It took fifteen minutes before things finally calmed down.

As a child, it was awful to see that display, and yet it was pivotal. At thirteen, that was a turning point for me. After that, I desperately wanted to play on my grandfather's team so that I could eventually play Ypsilanti and beat that team.

When the game was over, I shook their coach's hand and told him, "I will be back to haunt you."

Their coach smiled, patted me on the head, and said, "Okay, kid. Whatever."

COMMIT TO IT AND IT WILL COME

For five years, I visualized the moment I would get a chance to beat that team. I envisioned how I would feel and what that moment would be like. I could see my grandfather smiling, smoking his cigar, and being so proud of me—not only because our team finally went to the World Series, but because his grandson was the one to get us there.

Every day and at every practice, I visualized that moment. I played it over and over in my head. I was so committed to making that happen, I never took a day off from working toward that moment.

Five years later, I was pitching in the regional tournament. Ypsilanti was also there. I pitched in six games that tournament in relief and helped my team get to the regional final game against—yup, you guessed it—Ypsilanti!

To keep us from winning the championship, Ypsilanti would have to beat us twice. The first game, we were down nine to zero in the second inning. I remember sitting on the bench chomping at the bit to get into that game. We were saving our ace to pitch game two if we lost the first game. So when my coach came to the bench and asked if anyone wanted to pitch, I looked up and said, "Give me the ball, coach. This is personal."

I went out to the mound in the third inning, when we were down eight runs. The crowd was going crazy. My brother, one of those in the crowd, was screaming, "It's personal. Let's finish this!" I have never felt so out of body as I did in that moment. It was truly one of the greatest games I have ever pitched. I ended up throwing a no-hitter for the remaining innings and we beat Ypsilanti to go to the Connie Mack World Series.

Redemption!!! Me at age 18 (1991) pitching in the regional championship game to play in the Connie Mack World Series.

I could not believe my visualization came true. I walked over to the Ypsilanti coach to shake his hand.

This time, I stopped and asked him, "Do you remember me?"

He paused, his face turned white, and he said, "Oh, my God. You're that bat boy, aren't you?"

I smiled and said, "Yes, I am."

I shared this story with you because I want you to understand how committed I was, and how commitment can lead you to your dreams.

ONE DOOR CLOSES, ANOTHER OPENS

Even though we won that game, while at the World Series tournament I got some of the most devastating news I could have received—my grandfather was diagnosed with throat cancer. My happiness from that win quickly turned to sadness, and I lost my focus for the rest of the tournament. We ended up losing in the semifinals, and I felt my heart grow even heavier at the thought of having let down my grandfather, my mentor.

I was also distracted by the fact that I had a scholarship to Central Michigan University based on my courses of study, my musical talent, and sports, but with my grandfather's diagnosis I didn't know what I wanted to do. Everything seemed to be in chaos.

I ended up not going to Central Michigan, which was a crushing blow to my mother. I can remember sitting down with her getting ready to talk to her about my decision. My palms were sweaty and my face looked as though I was going to drop a bombshell on her, which I was. I had come to tell her that I was turning down a full ride to college—that I was not going right out of high school.

She had so much going on in her life at that time. Her dad was dying, her children were leaving the house and getting married, and she was broke. Now I had to tell her that I was throwing away my free ride to college to become a musician. Oh, and by the way, I pierced my ears as well. I remember feeling like I had failed her, but I knew if I did not follow my heart I would be making a decision based on her wants and needs, not my own. I explained to her that I had to do this.

Crying, my mom said that since she did not have the money to send me to college, she thought I was making a big mistake. But if I really felt strongly about it, she would back me in my decision. I told her I would never ask for a dime from her for my education, wherever I decided to go later, and I never did. (I did receive a lot of help on that journey, but I didn't have to rely on my mom, so I kept that promise.)

I also quit baseball altogether, a decision I still regret to this day—so much so that I have vowed never to quit anything again. But I don't regret it because of the path I'm on now—I regret it because I quit out of a fear of failing. Since I did not even try to pursue that path, I will never know where it might have taken me.

My grandfather passed away on February 3, 1994, roughly three years from the day he was diagnosed with cancer. I was working on a music career at the time and was pretty successful, but when he passed, I knew I had to do something to honor the man who had blessed my life.

My wife, Sabrina, started talking to me about the direction I wanted to go in life. As I related in the preface, I originally wanted to be a medical doctor, but Sabrina, who was a registered nurse, said she felt I would not be happy as an MD, because she knew how much family meant to me. She did not want me to be married to a pager my whole life.

Sabrina's words struck a chord with me, and I knew then that dentistry was my best option. I wanted to help people with throat cancer—I wanted to make a difference in someone's life and prevent them from getting the nasty disease that had taken my grandfather from me. I made a commitment from the moment my grandfather passed to make that difference.

Nine years later, I graduated from dental school and have been practicing ever since, with a focus on total wellness for my patients. It took a commitment on my part—more than just an interest—to get here.

WHAT'S THE DIFFERENCE?

There's a difference between being *committed* to something and just being *interested*. Let me ask you a few questions and see if you can tell the difference.

1. Are you interested in being a good person?

2. Are you interested in making lots of money?

3. Are you committed to achieving success?

4. Are you committed to doing something worthwhile in your life?

The four questions above will help you decide what is most important to you in this life and will help you define your purpose.

Your success in life depends on whether you are easily distracted by various interests, or whether you will stop at nothing to get what you want—it depends on the commitment level you give it. When I went to dental school, I did it with a wife and child. I was poor, working, and commuting over two hundred and fifty miles a day. I also had to fit in study time wherever I could, and on average I was sleeping four hours a night—and that went on for four years.

I was so committed to reaching my goals that my body worked on my behalf—almost on autopilot. I took those days one at a time, always keeping my focus narrow and keeping one eye on the finish line. When you are committed, you don't get distracted easily. You do what you have to do to get the job done.

If you only have an interest, you may start something, but you won't finish it. And if you have a setback or encounter a distraction that interests you more, you will quit that first interest.

Let's look at an example. How many people want to lose weight, say twenty pounds? They start out by eating right and exercising, but the weight doesn't come off fast enough and they quit. That is interest, not commitment. Imagine their success if they were committed. If they were committed to their goal and broke it down into workable parts, they would realize that by losing only ounces a day, they would success-fully lose that twenty pounds—in a year's time, they could lose even more. Someone who quits a weight loss plan before achieving their goal is not *committed* to a new lifestyle, they are only *interested* in losing a few pounds.

GET THE UNIVERSE INVOLVED

When you *commit*, the universe works on your behalf.

I was committed to beating Ypsilanti and I did it. I was committed to becoming a dentist and I achieved that goal with very little sleep and very little money. I got help from family, friends, and mentors along the way to reach my goal, because the universe will always reward committed people by putting people in your path to help you along the way.

We see marriages (and consequently families) break apart every day because someone decided to stop committing to the relationship. Somewhere along the way, two people forgot to commit to each other. They forgot that they had committed to their happiness. To be a good spouse, you have to commit to being a good spouse. To be a good parent, you have to commit to being a good parent. When you have moments with your spouse or when hanging with the kids, commit to those moments. Shut off the cell phone, avoid distractions. Be all in, fully engaged.

I have never in my life seen or heard of anyone who has committed and failed. I have seen many quitters fail, but never people who commit to something.

I have never in my life seen or heard of anyone who has committed and failed.

The pitcher Jim Abbott I talked about earlier went on to play for major league teams. He had a ten-year career and threw a no-hitter for the New York Yankees. He didn't get there by accident. He didn't let any setback derail him—he was committed to reaching his end goal.

When you truly commit, nothing stops you from reaching your goals. Commitment shows the universe that you believe in yourself, and that you have faith you will reach the end point and become a better version of yourself. The world will help you, and your subconscious mind will work on your behalf.

Are you afraid of success? No? Then commit and watch what happens in your life!

REASONS TO COMMIT

- Interest might get the boat rowing, but commitment will finish the race.
- Commitment makes everything stronger— relationships, yourself, and your wealth.
- Commitment is a contract with yourself. Don't break it. Sign on the dotted line to your destiny.
- Life is yours for the taking. Commit to your happiness.

CHAPTER 8

Pain of Discipline versus Pain of Regret

Once you start a task or set a goal, do you finish what you started? Do you stay the course until you get the results you want? Or do you take the easy way out just to get to the finish line? That's the difference between being disciplined and getting what you want in life and being undisciplined and wondering what could have been.

I believe there are only two pains in this world: the pain of discipline and the pain of regret. Successful people get where and what they want by being disciplined, by staying focused on their goals, and by not allowing anything to get in their way. Unsuccessful people tend to be undisciplined; they tend to be easily distracted and lose focus along the way.

You do not have to be the smartest person in the world to be a CEO, a doctor, a lawyer, a dentist, or other professional. But you must be disciplined. That's what separates people who achieve higher levels of education and people who have success stories to tell. It's not about intelligence, because let's face it, successful people include geniuses and some maybe not-so-smart people. But what does separate the winners is drive and discipline.

ADOPT A LASER FOCUS

When I was a student in high school, I was not the smartest guy in the room. As a matter of fact, grade-wise, I just got by. I did not march to the same beat as others, and I had attention-deficit disorder long before it was a common diagnosis. But the truth is, I simply did not care as much about school at that point in my life, and it had nothing to do with my ADHD. Since I didn't care, I didn't focus, so I didn't do well.

That changed by the time I entered dental school. In order for me to graduate dental school, I knew I would have to be disciplined. I had to devote every bit of my time to reaching my goal. I had to become laser-focused on my dreams and stop at nothing to achieve them. When my friends and family were celebrating holidays and going out to enjoy themselves, I was studying eight to nine hours a day in between working and raising a family with my wife. I could not stop for any reason, or my dreams would not come true. I slept about four hours a night for nearly four years to achieve my goal.

Still, I did not graduate with the highest honors. But my discipline allowed me to become the dentist that I am today, and it allowed my family to be blessed.

In short, my discipline was painful. But the pain of that discipline paid off. Had I not stayed disciplined and finished what I started, the result would have been the pain of regret.

How many times has someone lost a loved one and then wished they had one more minute just to tell the person how much they meant to them? Instead of waiting until that last minute, and then missing that opportunity in the end, why didn't they tell the person what they meant every day they were alive? Instead of being disciplined enough to say a few simple words every day, they end up living with the pain of regret—a pain that never goes away because they didn't take the time to tell someone how they felt.

EITHER WAY, THERE'S PAIN—WHAT'S IT WORTH TO YOU?

In order to really want something, you need to be willing to endure the pain that it takes to get it. Do you think a team that wins a championship doesn't work its tail off? Do you think an Olympic athlete doesn't sacrifice and feel pain? Think of Michael Phelps. He would get up while everyone was sleeping to go swim at four thirty in the morning in freezing cold water. He did that every day for four years. And what was the result? He not only won medals in the Olympics, he broke records. I don't know about you, but that kind of discipline seems more painful than fun. He could have easily taken days off and no one would have known, and no one would ever have questioned if he didn't hit his goal. But he knew. He would have lived with the pain of regret because he would have known that he did not give everything he had. He paid the price of discipline and now is an icon.

What if you could quit being disciplined without everyone knowing it? Would you do it? Take an offensive lineman in a football game. He could either stay disciplined and block his heart out or just turn his shoulders an inch, which would allow the defensive player to come in and sack the quarterback. The only other person who would know he quit would be the defensive lineman. He would carry the regret of his act, which may have cost his team a championship, for the rest of his life. Even worse, what if he did not block and the quarterback got hurt? He would have to live with that for the rest of his life.

The only thing that separates most people in this world is the way they live their life. People who stay disciplined tend to hold themselves to their morals and core values and never compromise on anything. But if you do not stay disciplined, you tend to lose some of who you are, and eventually you are stuck in what-the-hell-happened mode.

What would happen if our military did not stay disciplined? What separates the specialized ops like the Navy SEALS? They go through hell to become the best of the best. Why? So that they can protect us. They endure far more pain than the average person could ever endure. All they have to do is ring that bell and their life as they know it will go back to normal. Some do that. They can't endure the pain it would take to finish and become one of the baddest men or women on the planet. So they tap out and ring the bell, and they live with the regret of that decision for the rest of their life. The ones who endure the pain of discipline will forever know that they have everything it takes, and their confidence will be forever changed, because of the discipline they showed.

You can't get to the top without discipline. If you own a company, you have to sacrifice and stay disciplined to pay your bills, pay your employees, save money, and do the right things every day for the greater good of your business. Most companies fail because of lack of discipline. People tend to get too big for themselves, their egos get in the way, and they lose their focus and the discipline that made them great. That can be catastrophic, causing them to lose everything and live with regret.

You see, the pain of regret is the worst pain you can ever encounter.

You see, the pain of regret is the worst pain you can ever encounter. What if, instead of helping someone you see being bullied, you ignored what you saw? Then later you found out that the person committed suicide. Now you may live with that regret, that you did nothing to try and help that person, for the rest of your life.

Every one of us lives with deep regrets. We are not always proud of what we have done, and the crazy thing is, we never forget those instances. We never stop feeling the pain and are reminded of those decisions, or lack of them, every day. In contrast, I don't care about the pain it took to become a success story. I do not feel the pain of success every day.

Think of a woman giving birth. She has to stay disciplined for forty weeks, change her whole lifestyle of drinking and eating, and then endure a crazy amount of pain in order for a child to be born and bless her life. A mother who stays disciplined is rewarded at the end of that time with a new life, ideally a healthy life, that will change her world. But what about a mom who does not stay disciplined? She could lose the baby, or her actions could negatively impact the baby. An undisciplined mother may live with the regret of her actions for the rest of her life—and her child's life—while a mother who was disciplined and has a healthy baby forgets about the pain she endured once the baby is born. Some even go through it all over again. (I knew we were not created equal!)

If you truly want to be successful, or if you truly want to reach the best version of yourself, you must stay disciplined in everything you do. Don't go through life wondering what could have been and feel the pain of regret. Stay true to what you want. Stay the course and watch the greatness that can happen. Watch every relationship get stronger, watch your business grow, watch how other people respond to you. It will be life changing. And at the end of it all, the reward for all the pain you went through will be worth more than any money you could ever receive. Not doing this and living with regret will *kill you*.

BE DISCIPLINED—YOU WON'T REGRET IT

- To be the best version of yourself, you must be disciplined.

- Happiness starts with knowing what you want and staying disciplined in getting it.

- The pain of discipline is temporary, but the pain of regret lasts a lifetime.

- You only have one life to live—don't spend it living with regret.

CHAPTER 9

A Step in the Right Direction

A lot of people have no idea the direction they are going in life. They get on the hamster wheel of life, spin it around and around, and never go anywhere.

It's like someone stuck in the snow in their car. The wheels of the car spin and spin. Smoke billows from the engine; a lot of gas is used up. The person driving the car prays to get out of the snow—begs for a change in the situation in their favor. But still they go nowhere. They use a lot of energy, and then they have to call somebody for help anyway.

Throughout life, people may appear to be moving in the right direction, but years later they realize how much time they wasted doing useless activities. They never set a goal and established a starting point toward that goal. So at the end of the day, they went nowhere. People tend to move through life on autopilot, just going through the motions—hoping for change but changing nothing.

YOUR INTERNAL GPS

It is normal to have trouble navigating through life, especially if you don't really know what you want or where you want to go. But being open-minded and aware of your surroundings can help you determine your goals and reach your final destination.

When a destination is set on the map, we have tools to help us get there. Think about when you want to drive to a place you have never gone before. You get in the car and then call OnStar and ask for directions to your final destination. The GPS of your car navigates you throughout the journey, telling you when to turn left or right, whether there is a traffic jam or construction on your route, how much longer to your destination.

While our brains are not wired to take in the coordinates of where we want to go and then work on our behalf to get us there, you can create a plan that gets your subconscious mind to work as an internal GPS for you. That internal GPS can help

you navigate through life until you reach your destination—the fulfillment of your goals. Your subconscious mind can work exactly like that GPS system
in your car.

Programming in the destination of your internal
GPS is a matter of creating goals and then laying out
a detailed road map or plan of action for reaching
those goals. That's the first step in getting your life
headed in the right direction.

I can remember when I first applied to dental
school. I graduated with an undergraduate degree
from the University of Michigan, Flint, in 1997. My
plan was to go to dental school and graduate in 2002.
My plan didn't work out quite as expected, as I was
waitlisted for an entire year. Not only did I have to
wait, but I had to reapply. This cost me more money,
and there was no guarantee I would get the same
opportunity the next year. I knew I had to stick to
my plan of becoming a dentist, so I applied again,
even though I was broke, and managed to get into
dental school the following year. Thank goodness for
my wife, who kept me focused through the detour.

When I started, I thought, "Great, now it's full
steam ahead. No more roadblocks or detours for me!"
But I was so wrong. I now had to figure out how to
go to dental school, pay my house bills, support my

wife and child, and oh, by the way, study. I not only had to go to dental school during the day, but I had to work on the weekends. For a year, I worked third shift at GM. I commuted from Flint to Romulus and Detroit every day for nearly two years.

The journey was both emotionally and physically challenging. I can remember people telling me a year after I graduated how much better I looked. I chuckled and said, "Isn't having one job a good thing? So is sleep." I share this story because what seems like a straight path today may turn out to be a winding road tomorrow. Trust the GPS and stay the course.

Your subconscious will then create a game plan on your behalf for following that road map. How you control your thinking helps the mind know where you want to go and may even affect how long it takes to get there. Your thoughts will help get your subconscious GPS on the right path.

STAY THE COURSE

Just as when traveling in your car on a trip, your actual arrival time at your final destination is estimated. Sometimes you go with the flow of traffic, speeding up or slowing down. Sometimes you encounter construction or a roadblock—these can be frustrating, but if you stay the course or veer only slightly, you will eventually get to your destination.

The same is true when you set a plan in action with your mind. Once the GPS coordinates are locked and loaded, you can follow the plan to a tee. Your subconscious mind works on your behalf until you run into a roadblock—something happens in life to make you turn left instead of right, sending you off course. Getting knocked off course or off the intended path can happen for many reasons: a death in the family, a career change, someone needs your help. Whatever the reason, life happens.

The time it takes to reach your end point isn't as important as your willingness to stay the course, or to get back on course to finish what you started. Your GPS does not work without continued guidance, so sometimes you have to put in new coordinates and change a course. But at the end of it all, you will reach your final destination that you programmed into your subconscious GPS.

No matter how much struggle or chaos you go through along your journey, you need to

> **No matter how much struggle or chaos you go through along your journey, you need to stay close to the path that you set for reaching your goal.**

stay close to the path that you set for reaching your goal. Alter your course only if needed, but then get back on course as soon as possible to avoid getting lost along the way.

Too often in life, people allow other things to change the course they are on. Then they lack the discipline or patience to get back on track. Like getting stuck in traffic and resorting to road rage, it's too easy to let the negative take over when the path before you encounter a roadblock. Too many people just want to stop there and quit.

But if you look at those roadblocks from a different point of view, you may find that they actually saved your life. That's what detours in the road are for—they route you around a hazard. And in life, sometimes getting in a jam can be really helpful in actually figuring out which direction to take. The more positive or negative the emotions you give to a situation, the more of the same you get back. Your subconscious mind will feed you exactly what you are putting into it. So it can make a good situation great, or a bad situation worse. It goes only by the coordinates you give it.

TRUST YOUR INTERNAL GPS

When you find yourself getting off track from where you want to go in life, remember that everything you do is controlled by your thoughts and actions. For every place you want to go, you start by punching the coordinates into your internal GPS system. Whatever you tell it to do, it will then help guide you along that journey. It will help you get safely there as quickly as possible. Yes, there may be a roadblock or detour, but your mind and thoughts will take you to your final destination—just get them back on track.

An associate of mine got completely off track from his intended destination. He spent more time taking prescription drugs and drinking alcohol than he did working as a dentist. It got so bad that he even lost his license for writing prescriptions in other doctors' names. He ended up going to jail and was not allowed to practice for two years. His wife left him and took the children. I helped keep his practice going so that he could have some money coming in and not lose everything. That's when he decided to change. He started working out, got more focused on his needs, and reprioritized what was important to him. He stopped being afraid and faced the demons from his past. He broke free. Even though he took a totally crazy detour, he got help, got back on track, and is working again as a dentist. Hopefully he stays the course this time!

Sometimes you may find yourself at a crossroads, forced to choose between turning left or right. That's when you need to trust your internal GPS to help guide you in the right direction. Remember the end point of the journey—the more detailed and clear you are about that, the more your mind will work on your behalf to help get you there.

The journey will not be easy. As a matter of fact, it will be hell at times, but the universe will open up routes that will help you get there faster. It will even create new highways or avenues to help you reach your final destination.

Your internal GPS is the best in the business for you—no one else's GPS can guide you to your destination. Trust your own internal GPS, and it will take you places you never knew it could.

USE YOUR INTERNAL GPS

- Program into your internal GPS the coordinates of where you want to go in life daily.
- Double-check to ensure the coordinates align with your goals.

- If a detour comes along, have patience. It may be happening for a reason.

- Trust that you have the best GPS in the business and allow your subconscious to work for you on your behalf.

CHAPTER 10

Game Plan

Most people plan before going on vacation. They decide on a destination, purchase airline tickets and a hotel room, even research some of the food they might eat and sights they might see when they get there. All that planning gets them excited about something they're going to do for fun. And yet the same people struggle to plan for their future.

How often do you make plans? Do you plan your daily schedule? Do you plan out your weekly meals? How about planning for a year or even five years of life? Too many people go through life with no plan at all. How do you know where you are going without a plan?

If you want to accomplish your goals in the game of life, you need a game plan. You need to envision where you want to go in life. How many people do you know who go through life complaining that they haven't grown or seem stuck in a rut? That's because they lack goals, they don't have a plan for what to do with their life.

Think of a sports team—a football team, for example. They practice all week and set up a game plan before the game even starts. They determine what plays to run, and when they should run the plays in hopes of winning the game. They set up strategies based on who on the opposing team is playing in the game. Then they set up plays to counteract what they think the other team will do.

The game plan does not always work. When that happens, a good coach will tweak the game plan or make adjustments on the fly. The coach may even make drastic changes at half time, setting up an entirely new game plan. He or she does all that monitoring and guiding and planning just to win the game.

PLANNING GETS YOU TO THE TOP.

Working toward a goal in life is similar to setting up a game plan in sports. That's how top performers get to be top performers. That's how people win in the game of life—they put together a game plan. People who set a goal and move toward that goal usually finish ahead. And just as a game plan for sports doesn't always work and needs tweaking, so does a plan for life. Many times, we have to change our game plan or set up a new strategy if something isn't working. But the bottom line with people who win in life is that they have a plan and they follow it.

Planning and allowing a plan to evolve is how to grow and get better. Imagine if a coach never changed his game plan and every game was played the same. Eventually, every other team would know all the plays they were running, making it difficult for the team to win. Players on the team would get bored, stagnate, and eventually quit because they would feel like they weren't growing by winning and getting better.

When I think of evolving, I think of my own journey to becoming a better leader. When I first owned my practice, I thought everything was about me and my family. In my practice, I was more of a dictator—I just told people what to do. Then I realized that good leaders don't just tell people what to do. If your players don't want to play for you, you have no chance of winning the game. People must be coached. They need to understand the "why" of what they are doing.

As the years have come and gone while owning a business, I have realized that the game plan can change every day. It is how you adapt to the game being played that sets you apart. I evolve every day as a leader and business owner; I am constantly looking for new ways to improve. So business, and life, are about changing the game plan, if needed, and developing players who get you to the promised land.

The whole point of sports is meeting with resistance in order to continually get better. Sports teams must meet adversity—and even fail—in order to improve. They also need a lot of practice and repetition in performing the plays the right way to achieve perfection.

When you pursue your own goals, you first need to define what you want. You need to work on your craft daily in order to master it. If your goal is to be the top salesperson in the world, you need to study what has been proven to work. You need to practice cold calling, study your obstacles, and have a coach or mentor to help you along the way. Most importantly, years of practice and repetition will help you achieve your goal.

THE RIGHT TOOLS—MENTORS

You also need to have the right tools, or people, to help you work your game plan to perfection and a win. No one person alone can do everything—they need a team of people around them to help them reach their goal. Coaches have assistant coaches, a general manager, the presidents of an organization, salespeople, vendors, and others who support their efforts in managing the team. They also continually surround themselves with better and better coaches and support staff, and every year they draft in new members of the team—and sometimes cut lower performing teammates.

Some of my mentors during my development were my grandfather, my father-in-law, my wife, Dr. Paul Skoglund, Dr. Todd Engel, and entrepreneur Phil Hagerman. Not all of my mentors did the same thing. Some taught me dentistry, while others taught me to be a man. Dr. Skoglund, the best clinician I have ever known, reached out to me when I was not doing well in dental school. He told me that he had faith in me and saw something special in me. That had a huge impact on me, and to this day I'm not sure if he realizes just how much of a difference he made in my life. My wife is one of the biggest mentors in my life; she always guides me to become the best I can be.

That's the way to move closer and closer to your goal. Surround yourself with people who are better than you—people who are smarter, who are more experienced, who make more money. Too many people surround themselves with others who are not as smart as they are and who make less money. They do this to feel that they have the upper hand. That approach is all wrong. If you're the best player on a team, it is harder to get better. You won't be pushed enough, so you won't grow as fast. If you are at the top of the heap, you have nowhere to grow.

That's why it's often not the most talented player in high school who makes it to the pros. It's someone no one thought would make it—someone who had to work harder and grew as a result of determination, and then just kept growing and growing.

Too often people go through life in absolute chaos. That's because they don't have a plan for where they are headed, and they don't monitor that plan along the way. If you want to be the best version of yourself and win the game of life, you need to become better daily. Every evening, reflect on your day. Decide what worked and what didn't, and what you could have done better. That's what the best teams do.

I have a habit of debriefing every day. I always self-reflect on what I did right that day, and what I did wrong. I got this idea from watching and listening to other entrepreneurs. I saw that they carried a journal around, writing down goals, ideas,

> **If you want to be the best version of yourself and win the game of life, you need to become better daily. Every evening, reflect on your day. Decide what worked and what didn't, and what you could have done better.**

failures, successes, and just thoughts about the day. I realized that I must reflect on my day and identify ways to become a better leader. I spend about ten minutes a day just thinking of ways to be better. All great leaders do. They are working while others are sleeping.

Championships are not played by teams that win one game—they're played by teams that have won the most games at the end of the season. It's the same when following a game plan in life. It's not about one win, but a series of wins building upon each other, and at the end having a winning percentage that may put you in the hall of fame.

GET INDUCTED INTO THE LIFE HALL OF FAME

▫ Make a game plan for your journey.

▫ Surround yourself with more talented people.

▫ Become the best version of yourself.

▫ Reach for the championship.

CHAPTER 11
Take Action

Are you someone who relies on other people to get things done? Are you going through life not taking responsibility for what happens to you and to others? Many people just watch life pass them by, relying on others to solve life's problems. Even cities and cultures get stuck, never changing, because of a lack of action or a lack of accountability to the situation.

Many people are where they are because they don't take action for their life and dreams, and then they blame others for their circumstances instead of looking within themselves. They do the same thing over and over, expecting different results. Often that's said to be the very definition of insanity, but those same people will say they are not crazy (it's everyone else that's crazy).

ACTION STARTS WITH YOU

Truly changing your life path and accomplishing all that you want in life starts with you. You need to take action. You need to be responsible for your life. You need to take control of your outcomes without relying on others to do that for you.

Let's look at a struggling relationship. What are you doing to change the outcome? Are you the person in the relationship who thinks they are always right? Are you the one who waits for your spouse to say "I'm sorry" first or to say "I love you"? The problem with many failing relationships is that someone did not step up and take action first. Maybe investing back in that relationship could fix all of its issues. If one person would just take action and make the first step, then maybe the relationship would be a lot better.

Don't rely on others to fix your problems, and don't rely on others to react first.

Don't rely on others to fix your problems, and don't rely on others to react first. If you want that healthy relationship, then be the first to love and be the first to apologize. Be the first to make the plans. Take action and be a leader and watch what happens. Either you will get the results you are looking for or, if the relationship fails, you will know you did everything you could. Either way, you win. No regrets.

Whatever you want in life, it starts with you taking action. Once you get things in motion, then everything else can fall into place. If you want to be a doctor, it starts by taking the action of going to school. If you want to be an athlete, it starts by working your butt off training and practicing. If you want to invent something, it starts by allowing yourself to dream and then taking action. Yes, many people may help you along the way, but without you first taking action, you will not show the universe what you want and you will get no forward motion.

HOW TO SET GOALS

All this starts by setting goals. Without goals, you won't know where you are going or where you even want to go. You certainly will not know when you get there. You need to have goals in order to know if you were successful. You can't just think of what you want—you need to own what you want. You need to write out a specific plan of how to get there, and that plan needs to have set goals in order to keep the movement going. You need to take action and show the universe that you mean business, that you are not relying on others. Instead, you are taking action in your life to get the results you want.

So how do you set goals? How do you know if a goal is working on your behalf? Here are some tips for writing goals and helping you reach your goals.

Have well-defined goals. Write down exactly what you want and be as detailed as possible. Words are great, while visuals can take your goal setting to another level. If you want to own a business, consider: What does it look like? How many employees do you have? What is your product or service? How much are you going to make in a year? A business plan is a great tool for getting started in business—it will require you to think through every detail, including some you may not have considered.

Be specific. Success means different things to different people. You can't just say you want success without defining what that means to you. Be very specific in that definition. Does it mean financial stability? Does it mean being healthy and living to be a hundred years old? Again, the details matter.

Be realistic, but stretch yourself. When I set goals for my business, I always set goals that will stretch my staff and myself, but I never make those goals impossible to reach. I may want to increase my business by

50 percent, but that large of a goal may scare my staff off, and they may lose momentum on any smaller goals we've set—causing us to fall short. If you want to grow your business by 50 percent, set mini goals or have a game plan about how to get there to show your team how realistic the goal can be. Fifty percent growth is huge and may be too big of a stretch for a lot of people, so maybe a more realistic goal is to grow 25 percent each year and 50 percent over a two-year period. Either way, you are growing!

Make the goal sustainable. If you want to lose twenty pounds, that's a goal you can reach, but not in a week, and trying to do so would likely resort in the loss of some weight that you would put back on. After a week of starving yourself, you'd go right back to your old habits. But if you were to try to lose twenty pounds in ninety days, you might actually reach your goal. And you would do it in a way that would result in new, healthier eating and lifestyle habits—habits that you may sustain for a lifetime.

Make the goal worth your time and energy. Why do you think this is important? It's because if the goal is not worth your time and energy, you will not stay disciplined and committed to achieving it. You will only have an interest, and therefore the goal will lose its luster over time.

Write it down. If you don't write down the goals, your subconscious mind will not work on your behalf. When you write down your goals or, even better, tell them to someone else, you will hold yourself accountable to go and make them happen. You are committing to your future and showing the world what you really want. The more serious you are about reaching the goals and the more disciplined you are at making them happen, the more doors will open up for them to happen and the quicker they will come your way.

Read them out loud twice a day—at minimum. I start my day with an hour in the morning going over my goals, reading them out loud and aligning my thoughts to help make them happen. I also do this before I go to bed. If you pooled the top 1 percent of people in this world, I believe you would find they have a very similar practice.

Don't forget to celebrate when you reach your goals—and that includes mini goals. If your goal is to lose that twenty pounds in ninety days, then celebrate when you lose five pounds, ten pounds, and fifteen pounds. The reason this is so important is that it keeps your mind in a great place. Too often, we as a society do not celebrate growth or change the right way. We live in a world that tends to want to talk up the mistakes people make, their failures. If you don't have mini goals and celebrate them, it's easier to get discouraged and give up.

Stay the course and acknowledge how great you are! Remember, most people don't even take the time to know what they want in life, much less set goals. For goodness' sake, not everyone can even finish reading a chapter in a book that can help them grow. Congratulations, you are already a top performer and on your way to greatness!

BECOME THE LEADER YOU WERE ALWAYS MEANT TO BE

▫ Make sure you know where you are going and have a plan to get there.

▫ Write your goals down, read them aloud twice daily, and share them with other people to hold yourself accountable.

▫ Goal setting can be fun. It can help you dream. Allow your mind to work on your behalf.

▫ Take action and go get what is yours. Become the best version of yourself.

CHAPTER 12
True Character

We hear all the time about someone who has character. But what does that really mean? To me, character is the most important aspect of being human. Without good character or integrity, you can never be truly successful.

Character is the cornerstone of a solid foundation. It is the difference between being just an average person and being a person who stands at the pinnacle. Someone with great character will never compromise what they know is right. They will never do anything that may hurt someone else. Mostly, they will never do anything that would compromise who they are as an individual.

BE THE BEST YOU

Don't get me wrong. I am not saying you have to be perfect or that you must know what to do all the time. And, I'm not saying your character can never change. I am saying that you need to uphold your character the best you can and always improve yourself to become the best version of yourself that you can.

Can you imagine if you were reading a book or watching a movie and the character in it never evolved, never grew? Such a book or movie would be very boring—and likely a flop. People love stories and movies where the main character starts out as a complete loser or screw-up, but changes throughout the movie and grows to become a better version of themselves. They gain in confidence. They become a warm-hearted person. They change from being mean to becoming the most generous person they can be.

How many Christmas movies show an example of this? Scrooge, in *A Christmas Carol*, is the perfect example of the kind of character I'm talking about. He starts out as a man who is selfish, greedy, and alone. The ghosts of Christmas past, present, and future show him what life is like for others and how his life will turn out if he continues on his current path. As the story progresses, he feels his heart warm and realizes all the mistakes he has made throughout his life. His character changes—he becomes a nicer, more generous person, and his life becomes great as a result. By the end of the movie, the audience forgets everything about him being a jerk and greedy— they love him at that point. The audience leaves the theater with smiles on their faces and happiness in their hearts.

People respond in real life the same way when people change. I don't care about who you are today, but I do care about who you want to become. It has nothing to do with where you start—it is how you finish that matters. You could start out bad like my father, who was an addict early on but changed his ways to help other addicts as he got older. My father lives with a lot of regret, and I truly was embarrassed that he was my father, but I do respect what I learned from his mistakes, and I am thankful that he is clean and that he has changed his character to be a better person. He is trying to do good instead of bad, and I respect his change in character.

DON'T COMPROMISE YOUR CHARACTER

When you think of true character, think of Walt Disney and Mickey Mouse. You never ever see Mickey Mouse change who he is according to the situation he is in. You don't see him smoking ciga-rettes or drinking booze. You don't see him flirting with another mouse or pinching another mouse's bottom. Walt Disney wouldn't even allow T-shirts or other such items to alter the character of Mickey Mouse. He knew early on that if Mickey's character were compromised, the luster of Mickey Mouse would be lost.

How many of us go through life just like that? How many men and women behave differently around their spouses than they do around their friends? Do you talk to a man or woman the same way if your spouse is around than if they aren't? Do you behave the same whether someone is watching your behavior or not? Many people "fake it" at times or lie to themselves. Someone with true character will never compromise who they are, regardless of the situation.

True character is behaving the same way in public as behind closed doors.

True character is behaving the same way in public as behind closed doors. You can't be nice when the cameras are on but become a jerk when they're not. A lot of people hate religion because they think that people behave differently in church than they do at home.

The problem is, some people do. Even some pastors change who they are—they are someone far different in public than they are in person. Take Joel Osteen, for instance. Houston was in a crisis and many people were in need of food and shelter. Joel, a preacher who has written best-selling books and has received millions of dollars from his faithful followers, did not open up his church to those in need. He didn't open up his doors to the very community that loved and adored him. He got so much backlash that he eventually opened the doors—but that delay damaged his reputation. Instead of being the hero in a movie, people saw him as a villain.

Your character defines who you are and should align with your purpose. True character upholds you, not only with Christ but through the people you may be around or lead. People will always see that you're a fake if you don't have true character. You always have to be the same person in public that you are at home.

START WITH YOUR CORE VALUES

The thing that has helped me the most in becoming a person of true character is figuring out my core values. What are the core values of myself and my family? What are the characteristics I look for in myself? What are my weaknesses and my strengths?

Where do I need to grow? Here's an exercise to help you see whether you are a person of true character or whether you have some work to do. When you do this exercise, think about who you truly are and be honest with yourself.

DO YOU HAVE TRUE CHARACTER?

1. On a piece of paper, write down all your character traits. Ask yourself: Who am I today? Who do I aspire to become? This is your movie now.

2. Forget how you are starting out and focus on the character who is at the end of your movie. Think of someone you look up to. Maybe it is your wife or a family member. Maybe it is a mentor or a coach. Write out all of their positive traits and analyze whether you are close to them.

3. Once you figure out the traits you want to adopt as your own, work on them daily. If you are not honest today, never tell another lie. If you are not generous today, figure out ways you can be generous. The more you behave like the person you want to be, the more you become that person. Your character will

change over time to a better version of who you are.

RESIST TEMPTATION

A word of warning for people who are working on developing their character. Avoid at all cost situations that might compromise your character. I am a true believer in Christ, but I understand that Satan is right around the corner.

Don't allow yourself to even think of compromising your character. I liken it to a water dam. The dam can resist a lot of pressure and can stop the movement of water, but if too much pressure comes its way, the dam can break and let all that water loose, flooding everything below the dam. The same is true with situations that put you in harm's way with regard to your character. Avoid situations that put pressure on it to the point of breaking.

If you have no interest in drugs, don't hang around with drug dealers. If you don't drink, don't hang out in bars. These are not in line with your character. If you want to have a healthy relationship, don't hang out in strip clubs. Any act that pulls you away from your true character will have a dramatic impact on your development. Have you heard the phrase "If you put good in you get good out"? The same is true if you put bad in.

Ultimately, you're the one who will define your character. You will define the person you want to become and how you want to behave. Remember, to be the best you can be and live a happy life, you need to hold your character to the utmost standard and not compromise it for anything.

The best version of yourself will never be reached without a solid foundation of who you are and what you want to become. Be the difference maker in the story.

BECOME THE CHARACTER YOU WANT TO BE

- Write a list of the traits you want to adopt.

- Remember it is not who you are today, but who you will become. It is not how you start, but how you finish that matters.

- This story is *your* fairy tale. The character you have will help determine if you're the villain of the story or the hero. Choose to be the hero.

CHAPTER 13

Honesty

How many times have you heard people ask, "I wish he or she could only be honest"? But how many people can really handle it when someone is completely honest with them?

A lot of people go through life talking about honesty being a top priority. If you are one of those people, I caution you to be careful. If you are adamant on this stance, then you can't have a double standard. You can't get mad when someone is honest with you.

Guys, have you ever been asked by your wife whether an outfit makes her look fat? Our initial thought is, of course, "Oh crap, if I tell her she looks big, she will kill me. If I tell her she looks beautiful, she won't believe me anyway." Sometimes we wonder why we're even asked—we often feel there's no way we can win when such a question is posed.

With questions such as that, is the person asking because they really want your honest opinion? Or are they on some level looking to feel special or loved? Too many people really don't want or can't accept the truth. The truth is, to me, my wife is the most beautiful woman alive. I have never seen her look bad in an outfit. Well, maybe one. Seriously, I'm being honest! When it comes to women and their outfits, I believe they are looking for affirmation or confidence, not honesty. However, you can't lose character points if you're honest. You might sleep in a different bed, but in the end, your honesty will be appreciated.

THE HONESTY DOUBLE-STANDARD

But people, it seems, often have double standards when it comes to honesty. They want to be brutally honest to somebody and tell them things, but are not receptive when someone is being honest with them. In spite of what they say, many people really do not want to know the truth about the emotions someone else is feeling. On the flip side, is a person being honest if they really don't want to have a conversation about what is bothering them?

People have a hard time accepting accountability for their issues but can easily pass blame on everyone else. But nobody, and I mean nobody, is wrong 100 percent of the time (contrary to what your wife says, guys!). People can tell you to be honest with them but can't be honest with themselves. People can be very hypocritical when it comes to themselves.

Have you ever asked your boss to make changes knowing that your request was based solely on your own wants and not on the needs of the business? Have you ever said you're committed to a company's growth and then quit on them? In such instances, where was the honesty? Withholding information to only benefit yourself is not being honest, in my opinion.

Most people travel through life being honest when it can't hurt someone. For example, everyone says every baby is pretty, but the reality is that there are a lot of ugly babies—so we may be dishonest when admiring a child. Sometimes others ask for our opinion, but to avoid hurting their feelings, we are dishonest with them. "Do I have wrinkles?" "Do I look fat?" "No, you look great!" How many times has someone asked you to guess their age and you've shaved off a few years out of a desire to avoid offending them? That's being dishonest.

The truth is, people don't want to hurt other people—and that is a great thing. However, you can't have double standards. If you want someone to be honest with you, you can't condemn them when they *are* honest. Your response to their honesty has to be encouraging. You need to thank them for their honesty and tell them you respect it. It's okay not to agree, but it's not okay to be mad at them for being honest.

> For those who struggle with honesty, the more honest you are in every situation, and the more you are able to be accept honesty, the more you improve your overall character.

For those who struggle with honesty, the more honest you are in every situation, and the more you are able to be accept honesty, the more you improve your overall character. And it gets easier with practice. It's like working out; at first, it's hard, but you get into a pattern and groove, and then it becomes easy.

A person who is honest is not cocky, or arrogant, like so many people think. They are a genuine person who is giving you feedback to aid in your growth. Accept it for face value and move on to become a better version of yourself.

It might not seem like it, but *you never lose by being up front and honest.* But *you can lose everything you ever wanted or owned if you are dishonest.*

HONESTY IS YOUR BEST FRIEND

▫ It helps you establish trust with people.

▫ It gets you closer to the character you want.

▫ When you are honest with yourself and others, you are becoming the best version of yourself.

▫ When you are honest, it just feels better. Think of how you feel when you tell a lie.

▫ Honesty is a true sense of leadership.

CHAPTER 14

Leadership and Self-Awareness

One of my favorite authors on leadership is John Maxwell. A lot of this chapter is my take on concepts from his book *Good Leaders Ask Great Questions*. He has helped me become aware of my strengths and weaknesses throughout my growth as a leader.

First of all, what is leadership? According to Maxwell: "Leadership is influence," and the ability of one person to influence others to follow his or her lead. Let me add to that: A great leader knows when to lead but also knows when to follow. A true leader is as good a follower as he is a leader.[1]

---

1   John C. Maxwell, *Good Leaders Ask Great Questions: Your Foundation for Successful Leadership* (New York: Hachette Book Group, 2014).

Most of the time, people are not naturally born as leaders. They may have the ability to lead, but leadership is more of a learned skill than an instinct. Just as I could never be a great dentist in dental school on the first day, it is nearly impossible to be a natural born leader and be perfect at it. Leadership is more of a learned behavior that you master over time. As Maxwell explains it, people start out as babies, then grow to become good leaders, then grow to become great leaders.

Leaders can have a tremendous influence on people, whether a good influence or a bad influence. There is not a day that goes by that I don't fail in leadership on some level—not a day that I couldn't have done something better, something differently, to be a better leader. I don't know what it takes to become a master at leadership, but I do believe you can influence people in a positive way every day and help them grow. To me, that defines a great leader— placing your needs secondary to someone else's growth. That is a step toward being a great leader. Not one person is perfect, but if you work on leadership daily you can become the GOAT (greatest of all time) at leadership.

LEADER—KNOW THYSELF

Being a great leader starts with knowing yourself, loving yourself, and being the best version of yourself. You also need to know your core values and what you hold to the highest standards, and never compromise. You can't expect people to follow someone who doesn't know what they want. Leaders must be aware of their strengths and weaknesses. You really need to know how you think and behave. One of my biggest obstacles as a leader is to keep my composure in all situations. I don't like when people question my intentions or character. It creates a lot of anxiety for me, and when I feel that way, I sometimes allow emotion to creep in and take over. That is poor leadership, but because I am aware of my weakness, I can fix it and change my behavior over time and become the best leader I can be.

A true leader is someone who can change and become better. To be a true leader, you must always be getting better. First, you've got to *want* to become a better leader. Then, you must work on developing yourself to become better daily. It takes a lot of energy and time to really know yourself. Also, remember that leader-

> **A true leader is someone who can change and become better.**

ship is a challenging aspect to undertake. It can change day to day, so what makes you unique today can make you ordinary a different day. That is one reason to understand who you are and be aware of your strengths and weaknesses.

What if you can't change your weaknesses? Then surround yourself with people who have different strengths than you do. Surround yourself with people who can make your weaknesses into strengths. People will follow someone who is vulnerable, and when you know your strengths and weaknesses, you will be more comfortable knowing your vulnerabilities as well. Also, look to other leaders and mentors to help make you a better leader. The fact that you are reading this book shows that you want to improve. John Maxwell has created several books on leadership, and there are a lot of other people to help you develop as well.

THE LAW OF RECIPROCATION

You don't have to be a CEO of a company to be a leader. All you need is a desire to make a difference. Let's say you want to help people. In that case, you first need to believe in them. Just as a person has to believe in a leader in order to follow, a leader must believe in the people they want to lead. It is the law of reciprocation. If you want to have people follow and help you along your journey, you need first to believe that they are great and want to help you.

Leadership does not always need to have a big, inflated title. You can lead by being the best in the job you have. Leadership is earned, not entitled. You can change a process in a way that has never been thought about. You can change the way a business runs. You can help create a new culture in a business. True leadership can happen anytime and anywhere.

Recently, I saw the movie *12 Strong*, about twelve Green Berets after 9/11 and how they help take down the Taliban. The main character was loved by the eleven other Green Berets, but he never killed anybody and never fought in a war. He was just a great strategist, and people gravitated to him. He was always thinking outside the box and did not beat to the same drum as everyone else in the military. He made commitments and kept them. He did not take no for an answer, and he always finished what he started. No excuses. He was a great leader. That was not even the best part of the story. The movie also did a great job of showing how a leader has to be the first into battle and sometimes has to do some crazy stuff. It also showed that even as a leader, sometimes you have to follow. It was one of the best movies I have ever seen with regard to leadership.

TRAITS OF A LEADER

Sometimes when people think of leadership, they think of a dictator. That is not leadership—that is someone with an ego thinking they are leading. This is one of the hardest struggles as a beginning leader. Beginners think leadership is telling people what to do and how to do it. That is the furthest thing from the truth. True leadership is teaching people what to do and helping them see the best way to get there. Allow the people working under you, or with you, to develop a process that works for them. At the end of the day, it is about results. Your team needs to buy into what you are selling. The quickest way for that to happen is to allow their strengths to shine and help nurture and mentor them to become leaders themselves.

The best leaders are also visionaries. They have strong intuition, can see a problem arise before it exists, and can think out of the box to come up with solutions. They know the exact buttons to push for movement, and they know when to pull back to slow the ship down. They are willing to take risks on their own. They can adjust their plan when things don't go as planned and can maintain calm—even laugh—in a crisis situation. They see the positive in life and don't take things too seriously.

When I think of leadership, I think of people who lead without even knowing they are doing it. They are the people that everyone instantly wants to rally around. One of the greatest leaders I know, whether she knows it or not, is my wife. Sabrina has a way of coming into a room and shining. People will follow her in whatever she does. I often reflect on and am in awe of how wonderful a leader she is. She is not afraid to be brutally honest, and she goes out of her way for the greater good of other people and her family. She truly is the leader of our home. She allows others to shine when she is in the background. She knows when to follow to let others lead. She also holds people and her family to high standards of character. She does not compromise who she is, even if she has to stand alone at times. She is the true embodiment of leadership to me.

True leaders also have a greater purpose. They are selfless, asking questions such as, "How am I helping my team?" instead of, "How am I benefiting?" They know when to take the accolades, and when to give them. A true leader puts their team ahead of themselves and lets others shine. A leader knows that it is more rewarding when a teammate gets an award than when they do themselves.

___

Here are some of the qualities of a leader, according to John Maxwell. How many do you have?

___ is influential

___ has self-discipline

___ has a good track record (good character)

___ has strong people skills

___ is a problem solver

___ goes above and beyond

___ sees a bigger picture

___ is a positive person

___ understands people

___ is free of personal problems (the hardest one, in my opinion)

___ is willing to take responsibility

___ is free from anger (I fail in this one sometimes)

___ is willing to make changes (one of my strengths)

___ has integrity (most important, or at least one of the most)

__ sees what has to be done next

__ is accepted as a leader by others

__ is willing to keep learning

__ is charismatic

__ has good self-image (most people struggle
    with this one)

__ is willing to serve others

__ is resilient

__ can develop other people

__ takes initiative

__ pursues excellence

———————————————————

To become the best leader you can be, it is important to work on being all of these things.

Everyone has leadership qualities, and anyone can become a leader. Today I want you to make the choice to become that leader. Make a decision today to lead no matter the situation you are in. Be that leader in your workplace, at home, at your church. Be the best you can be.

We were not put on Earth to be anyone's puppet. We were not meant to always follow. We were put here to be the best version of ourselves that we can be. You cannot be that by always sitting in the back of the bus, or by always allowing others to run your life. As Patrick Swayze says in the movie *Dirty Dancing,* "No one puts Baby in a corner." Take the lead of the final dance. Take the lead in your journey of life. When you do, you will realize how much people will follow and help you along the way,

BE THE BEST *YOU* THAT *YOU* CAN BE!

- In order to be a leader, you must be aware of who you are.

- Surround yourself with people with different strengths than you have.

- You must follow at times in order to become a great leader.

- You must be selfless in order to be a great leader.

- Leadership is a forever changing situation. You must adapt to every person and situation.

- Never stop becoming the best you can be. When you stop growing, you stop being a great leader.

CHAPTER 15

Faithful Wavering

What is faith? It is believing something is going to happen before it does. Faith is already planning to be successful before reaching that pinnacle. Faith is commitment. Do you have faith—faith in a higher power, faith in yourself, faith in your kids, faith that whatever situation you are in will get better?

Have you ever noticed that your faith wavers— do you have faith only when things are going well, or only when things are at the lowest of lows? Too often people say they have faith when things are going well, but not when things are going poorly. Why is their faith lessened? When things go well, we tend to take all the credit, but when things go bad, we blame others—we rarely blame ourselves.

True faith is like confessing your future before it happens, believing beyond a shadow of a doubt that it will happen. Fear is the opposite of faith. Most people don't really have faith, because they are always fearful of loss or failure. Do you really have true faith if you have fear in your heart? The answer is no!

You should fear nothing if you truly have faith. You should never fear death, because heaven

> **You should fear nothing if you truly have faith.**

is supposed to be true life, not what is here on Earth. You should never worry about failure, because each failure helps you learn and gets you to where you want to go. You need to have faith that everything you are doing is for a better reason—for you and a bigger plan.

We are all called to fulfill a purpose. We have responsibilities to also serve the Lord. You have to understand that things are happening for a reason, and you need to have faith, no matter what. We are not only living a life on Earth, but we are living a life for our Savior. Everything you do is not only for yourself, but for the bigger plan in life and eternal life.

Let's talk about a person who applies for a job. Do they go into the job interview with so much confidence because of their faith in getting the job? Or are they not even qualified but are fooling themselves that they can get the job? Have they already envisioned what the job would be like—what they will wear to work, the décor and floor plan of their office, their various responsibilities? Most people do not have a faith so strong that they think this way, or they didn't think of the situation in this much detail. Often they don't truly believe they deserve the job, or don't have strong enough faith that they will get it.

Faith changed my life less than ten years ago, before I was an owner of a multimillion dollar business. I had just sold a practice in Clawson, Michigan, and was working as an associate at Gateway Dental in Flint. I can remember the feeling when I first walked into the practice, and I knew then that this was where I was supposed to be. This truly was the place that was meant for me! It was as if the owner had built the floor plan in the vision I had always imagined. It was a big practice, but warm and welcoming, and it was *home*.

I was only working one day a week at Gateway, and the practice was built in 2001. The owner wasn't planning on retiring anytime soon, so he wasn't planning on selling anytime soon.

I started praying and having faith that I was going to own this practice. I started changing the floor plan to how I would have it, and I started acting differently to the staff and patients. I truly was acting as if I were the owner of the practice even though I worked there only one day a week.

The Lord will give you anything you want, as long as you have faith and work toward it first. I was studying this place inside and out. I was analyzing which employees were trustworthy and which employees were selfish and only about themselves. I knew everything, down to the labs and supply costs.

I also remember going up to the owner and proclaiming, "I will own this practice!" I truly believed I would own it. Every time I asked if he was going to sell, he would say no.

I was there for six months. Then one day, in June 2008, the owner of practice actually came up to me and said, "I don't know why I am asking you this because I never was going to sell this practice, but are you still interested in buying Gateway?" I was trying to play it cool, but on the inside, I was screaming: "*Hell yeah!*"

A few months later, in September 2008, I bought the practice—three months before the economy crashed. And at that point, I had only $20 to my name Ten years later that $20 has become a multi-million-dollar dental practice, with a second location in Swartz Creek, Michigan. That all led to motivational speaking and this book! So you see, you can't stop the power of faith, or the power of the Lord. He will remove all obstacles in your way, and make sure you get what is meant to be yours—as long as you have *faith*. I trusted, took a giant leap of faith and here I am, ten years later, running a hugely successful practice with a team of individuals I love. I believed it would be this way, and it is!

IT'S ABOUT FAITH

▫ It's okay if your faith wavers occasionally. It's only human to lose trust or confidence when this happens, but you need to get back on board with faith. Live more in faith than not.

▫ You must have so much faith that you will get what you want that you commit to it. If you are sick, have faith that you are already better.

▫ You must have faith and believe you are worth the blessing coming your way. You can't fool the man upstairs.

CONCLUSION

I'm one of the most fortunate people in this world, and I pushed through thick and thin to get where I am today. I think back to the situations and circumstances that made me who I am, the people that forged me into a believer that hard work and immense effort will get you places if you just try.

Stop what you're doing and think. Look around you. Consider the next steps in your life and where you want your feet to land. Will your game plan be just to better yourself? Who are you impacting with your decisions? Is it your parents—your wife and children? When you take action, know that you can't be selfish, and know that there'll be roadblocks at every twist and turn. Despite these setbacks, optimism and courage are your allies.

When I was younger, I obsessed about any roadblocks that were in my way. I made it my life's duty to get through what held me back from success, and as I grew, I made sure that I can help my family overcome those roadblocks and find their own success. I don't want my children to have to go through the same struggles I did, but at the same time, I want them to be humble, to be honest and faithful.

That's why I practice what I preach in this book. I want anyone who is going through both hard times and good times to be prepared for whatever life throws at them. My job has to be the best in the world for this, because not only am I helping my patients physically by improving their health through dentistry, but I also get to develop meaningful, long-lasting relationships with them and even their families. I get to talk to them one-on-one and do my best to support them in their endeavors, whether they are children aspiring to be the next astronaut or adults who are about to make a huge career move.

I believe we all have a choice in where we find ourselves in our lives. There are opportunities everywhere, waiting to be seized, whether they are huge leaps in your life, or just small steps. The only thing that will hold you back is *you*. If you are the best you can be, then you can overcome anything that you think may be setting you back. You don't have to inherit the destinies of those that came before you.

It's up to you to forge your own path, and perhaps, once you have found satisfaction, you can help change other's lives as well.

ABOUT THE AUTHOR

Bobby J. Grossi graduated high school from Flint Powers Catholic in 1991, received a bachelor's in science from the University of Michigan Flint in 1998, and graduated from the University of Detroit Mercy School of Dentistry in 2003 with a doctor of dental surgery degree.

He currently resides in Linden, Michigan, with his beautiful wife and best friend, Sabrina, and is the proud father of three: son Brayden, and daughters Andelina and Zandria. He owns and operates two dental practices and is the co-owner of Great Lakes Dental Design. He founded the Grossi Institute for dental assisting in 2016, where he currently teaches. He enjoys motivational speaking and writing.

He lives by his philosophy of, "One pitch at a time," which focuses on living in every moment and enjoying life to the fullest. Through many successes and failures, which he is never afraid to share, he has evolved into a person who leads by example. He stays open to critical feedback through keeping an open mind and is willing to take major risks to accomplish his goals.

Dr. Grossi actively leads his business teams, is a very in-the-moment father, and coaches his travel baseball teams, a high school baseball team and his daughter's softball team. He is guided by his purpose of helping others and realizes that life is not about him—it's about the impact he has on others and the legacy he wants to leave behind.

"My purpose is to try to improve the lives of every person I come into contact with and try to mold the kids I coach into better young men and women."

—DR. GROSSI

Printed in the USA
CPSIA information can be obtained
at www.ICGtesting.com
JSHW012035140824
68134JS00033B/3075